HIKING

TO BEER

HIKING
TO BEER

A MEMOIR

LLOYD FINK, JR

NORTH LOOP BOOKS
MAITLAND, FL

NORTHLOOP
PRESS

North Loop Press
2301 Lucien Way #415
Maitland, FL 32751
407.339.4217
www.NorthLoopBooks.com

ISBN-13: 978-1-63505-270-1
LCCN: 2016954183

Printed in the United States of America

Foreword
By: Ryan Magaro

The Appalachian Trail runs some 2,190 miles from Georgia to Maine. Since the first quarter of the 20th century the Appalachian Trail has drawn people to its white blazed pathways. Some out for a day hike. Others for a few days or weeks. But for others, there is a fire that once ignited can't be quenched until they journey its entire length.

If you have ever spent time on the trail you know that there are people from every walk of life, age, background, and mental state! A trip on the AT guarantees you will meet new and interesting people that may or may not share your views on politics, religion, nutrition, and even personal hygiene! What they do share is an idealistic quest to come back to nature and conquer the elements and their own limitations. I like to say that everyone on the AT is hiking **to** or **away** from something.

Lloyd "Uke" Fink is one such trail character that is larger than life. I like to claim that I introduced Uke to hiking in our early teenage years. We grew up together in the mountains of North Central Pennsylvania in the small town of Emporium. Emporium means "Center of Trade". The Native Americans used the steep river valleys to portage canoes from the Allegheny River to the Sinnemahoning Branch of the Susquehanna for thousands of years. It is a fitting name for this idyllic community nestled in the great green valleys of Cameron County. We took for granted the hundreds of miles of secluded dirt roads and seldom used hiking paths that covered the landscape. I liked to hunt and fish and Lloyd liked to do anything new. We began hiking together up the 1000 foot mountain affectionately known as "the mountain behind my house". This steep mountain is scarred with the remnants of the logging industry that brought many to the area in the 19th century. On one occasion our ignorance caused us to have an awkwardly cold night on the mountain. My father had some camping gear but it would not be qualified as 3 or 4 season. This did stop Uke and I from attempting a great late winter camping expedition. If this trip would have happened now it may be grounds for Children and Youth Services to pay our parents a visit. However in the early 90's it was a wild time where kids spent every daylight hour outside, and at the creek. We would climb this mountain as teenagers unaware of the impact hiking would have on both of our lives.

Fast forward a few years and our lives took different paths. I was always a regimented, rule following, straight edge, kind of guy. Uke was always a free spirited, go where the wind blows, always up for an adventure sort of fellow. As I began working he began exploring the country by any means possible. We would talk once in a while but slowly our two paths drifted apart. I got married to my smoking hot wife Brandi in 2004. Over the next few years we had our three children Enzo, Milla, and Aria. And as time went on we settled into our married with children routine. In 2012 Uke came back into our story.

My sister moved to Culpepper Virginia in the fall of 2012. She and her husband needed some assistance getting the furniture up to the second floor. While there our old friend Uke showed up from his place in nearby Fredericksburg and did all the heavy lifting. We chatted for a while getting caught up on the years that had passed us both by. He mentioned he was training for an upcoming hike on the Appalachian Trail. I am sure I had a look of surprise as soon as the words came out of his mouth. Like all of us, Lloyd had put on a few pounds over the years. He was always a hulking figure but now he was pushing 350 pounds. I didn't know much about the AT at the time but I did know that it was a long trail that wasn't for the faint at heart. As always Uke was never afraid of a challenge. Heck, he was never afraid to challenge things like "logic" and "reason". We parted ways that night and we watched, via social media, Lloyd transform from a boulder sized man into a lean, mean, hiking machine. This chance visit created a spark in me.

As the months passed Uke hit the trail. We followed his progress with amusement. Day by day this amusement changed to awe as he progressively increased his mileage, shed the pounds, and got closer to the midway point on the trail. The idea that he might actually be able to do this started to sound less like a child's innocent dream and more like reality. The spark in me turned into a flame. We discussed getting together as he passed through Pennsylvania. By that time he was crushing miles and our path wouldn't be able to cross as hoped. Our family vacation that year was in Massachusetts and by chance the timing was going to be pretty close to allow us to meet up with Uke. We began planning. I would meet up with him on Mt Greylock and we would jump off in Bennington, VT and pamper him with food, a much needed shower, and 3 wild children who were excited to see him. The flame for me grew into a fire. As Uke continued on the lure of the AT had hit me hard. I knew I would never be able to through hike (at least not until my children are grown) so I decided to start a very long term section hike. Uke and I discussed the possibility of a Katahdin summit prior to the Mid October closing of the park it resides in. The time came and this became a reality. My father in law jumped in for the 17.5 hour drive to Maine and we picked up Uke and headed for Millinocket. We couldn't have asked for a more beautiful day to climb the northern terminus of the AT. I was privileged to watch as Uke and many of the through hikers I had met in Vermont finished their journeys. Although Uke had a few more miles to go he had, for all intents and purposes, reached the goal. I now had a respect for Lloyd "Uke" Fink never present in our years of friendship. He accomplished something only 1 in 4 who set out each year complete. An epic adventure. A Herculean task.

Sit back and enjoy this tale told in Uke's honest and whimsical style. Share in his up's and downs. Share in his failures and successes. Share in the experience that is the Appalachian Trail.

Chapter ONE

Leaving things behind has never been hard for me. I enjoyed roots in Fredericksburg, Virginia, for many years. Several things were keeping me there. I was working as a paraprofessional with at-risk youth for over nine years in a day-school setting. The work with these kids was difficult, yet rewarding.

Unfortunately, the school program was terminated in the summer of 2011. My life felt as if I were trapped. My anxiety was elevated and depression was becoming an issue. I was not satisfied. Something in my life did not feel right. So, I tried planning a different approach toward life on this big blue ball.

My doctor was concerned about my health and suggested that I exercise more and eat better foods. My weight was a concern to him, at approximately 350 pounds. My blood pressure was a red flag, as well. He explained to me that if I could not get the problem under control, then I would need to take medicine for it. I was pretty much going to run a slow race out of this world, and I needed to make a change.

In late August 2012, on a beautiful Virginia summer day, I was given an epiphany. My friend Larry's friend, Bill, stopped by the Hinkle Ukulele Workshop in Stafford, Virginia. Larry and I were having coffee after a glorious night of much debauchery. Larry's friend was telling us that he needed to send his son new boots in Connecticut.

"Why are you sending your son boots?" I asked curiously.

"My son is hiking the Appalachian Trail, headed southbound, and his other pair got worn out," he replied.

"Wow, I would love to do that!" I exclaimed.

"Then you should," he said without sounding snarky or with any hint of sarcasm in his voice.

Larry believed I could accomplish, or at the very least attempt to perform, the mammoth journey. I have to admit, having both of them look at me with confidence was encouraging. As I sat there at Larry's outside table, a fresh summer breeze indicating the beginning of the Virginia fall season, sipping on some delicious black coffee, I made up my mind.

"I'm going to quit drinking beer, quit smoking cigarettes, and I am going to hike the Appalachian Trail!" Again both guys were gung ho for my enthusiasm.

The reason I decided to quit drinking beer was because I love beer. Like a carrot on a stick, attached to a rabbit, beer would become my carrot.

They knew I was capable of the challenge. That was a big deal for me. I wasn't sure if I wanted to continue in the field of mental health due to the extreme behaviors I sometimes witnessed with the clients. I was drinking alcohol irresponsibly and not taking care of myself as I should. Determined to set the goal, the hamster on the wheel was moving.

"I'll build you a brand new ukulele to take with you on your journey, a Hinklele!" Larry offered to add a bit more motivation for me to realize this dream.

We all sat back and enjoyed a few laughs at how Larry's last name, Hinkle, and the word "ukulele" fused together to make it roll off the tongue, a Hinklele.

There is planning in walking over two thousand miles. It would be at mile five hundred where I would be bitten by a very dangerous spider, twice. And if it weren't for my family and close friends, I would not have even realized the end purpose: hiking from Georgia to Maine along one of America's oldest hiking trails, the Appalachian Trail.

When I started my training, I could not bend and touch my toes, nor could I touch my nose to my knee due to my enormous tummy. It was, for me, an excessive burden.

Training for the journey began on September 1, 2012. My friend, Sarah, who manages a superior fitness and training business in Virginia, offered me suggestions on how to prepare for my hike. I explained to her my goal and she was helpful in giving me pointers to be productive and safe. I began walking five miles every day with ten pounds inside my backpack for the first week. I would take weekends off to rest. The following week I upped the mileage by one mile and the poundage by five pounds. Once I reached around forty-five pounds, I was hiking approximately thirteen miles every day! Certain days when my body was yelling at me, I would do less, but I was unfailing in my routine.

There are many great hiking areas around Fredericksburg, Spotsylvania, and Stafford, Virginia; I made use of in my training. Pratt Park in Stafford was the area I liked to use more than others. In the mornings, I would wake up before sunrise to catch it while I hiked around the park. I had a few run-ins with skunks at this early hour, and although I was nervous getting within a few feet of them, I did not let that distract me from finishing my daily mileage. I also used several Civil War battlefield trails in and around Spotsylvania. When I was doing bigger miles, I hiked from Spotsylvania, through the city of Fredericksburg, and into Stafford. I used this trip as a rule to my future mileage goals.

My friends and family were all very encouraging to me. For my birthday, my Aunt Gin and Uncle Tim got me a book by Paul Stutzman called *Hiking Through*. It is a very inspirational book, and Paul completed the five million steps from Georgia to Maine. When attempting something as mammoth as hiking the Appalachian Trail, it's important to find stories and books of folks who inspire us to the finish. After reading and watching some tutorial videos online, I felt confident when my first footsteps hit the AT dirt. The proverbial ball was rolling, and my initial tasks were much more enjoyable.

I researched types of meals to eat while out in the wilderness. Perhaps I would ensnare a squirrel or two, or maybe catch a grouse to roast over an open fire pit. Rub the meats with ramen packets. Mainly the homemade meals I made were oatmeal with some individual ingredients, mixed rice and beans with an added protein, such as a tuna packet, and so much granola and trail mix that I would tire of chewing the stuff.

My work during this transition was with a local group home. The schedule I was on was primarily weekend double shifts. I gave my manager a heads up three months in advance and a well-worded letter of my intentions. My job with these young men on the weekends was sporadic to say the least. When I arrived at work, I would read behavior reports on the clients from the previous week. Weekday behaviors differed from weekend acts because the weekend expectations were not as strict, due to a more stringent school schedule. Some behaviors I witnessed and reported on ranged from smoking cigarettes to running away. My goal in the time that I worked there was to find common ground with the clients. I was well versed from decisions I made as a troubled young kid, myself. Once I found the common ground, I attempted to show them how to work for certain privileges by completing their household chores, demonstrating respect to their peers and staff, and also having control over their negative traits. A big thing the clients saw in me was that I cared. I did not attempt to be their friend. I gave clear and concise directives and was never afraid to tell them "no." Sure, they tested me. They were aware I was going to do what I said I was going to do, whether it is was a negative consequence or a positive result. When Sunday night rolled around, I was off for several days. That gave me time to hike . . . train.

After I had researched gear, I bought a used air mattress. My cousins, Jennifer, Robby, Robyn, and Lucas, got me a reliable headlamp, and then I got myself some cheap trekking poles to take some stress off of my weak knees. The next purchase was an excellent backpack. Then I got a pot and stove to cook with. My friend, Greg, who has been a father figure to me since I was a little shit, sent me a wind-up radio to listen to the weather forecasts and a box of "add hot water" meals. I made a bunch of my meals, as well. I sent the packages general delivery to the post offices along the trail[1].

---

[1]   A route made across a wild region, over rough country, or the like, by the passage of man or animal. A trail differs from a path in that a path tends to be a convenient means of foot travel to avoid roads. A path serves in place of a road, takes you between two civilized localities. A trail takes you away from civilized things.

The most important thing I read and researched about was "take care of the foots!" My friends, Chris and Adrienne, also reiterated this to me during a get-together at their home in Culpeper, Virginia. I would learn quickly how to feel for red flags regarding my feet. I already had poor feet when it came to calluses and a natural toughness for the rigors of the trail.

One time I was hanging out with a friend and my sock had a hole in it at the heel. My friend looked down at my foot and asked, "Why do you have shoes on underneath your socks?" That's how horrible my feet were. We both shared a laugh, but then he asked again, "Seriously, those aren't shoes? That's your foot under your socks? Dude? That is the weirdest thing I have ever seen!" My blister prevention on the non-calloused areas of my feet was super glue and moleskin. It would prove invaluable.

---

* I needed my hike to mean something for other people, as well. Because I had just left a profession in mental health, I researched mental health and hiking and came upon the organization, HIKE for Mental Health. I could hike for them and put it on my social media sites for tax-deductible donations. I thought hiking for a cause may help people who suffer from a mental issue. I was happy hiking for a cause . . . that, of course, and beer.

A month before leaving Fredericksburg, I gave my body a rest from training. My friends and past coworkers, Mollie, Sharon, and Melissa, had a going away party for me at a local Mexican restaurant. We laughed and talked about old times working at the day school. We felt saddened that it was closed down after the progress the school was showing. It was unfortunate, and we all agreed that the kids would grow up and, fingers crossed, become successful members of society.

My mind and body were seated in this goal of hiking the Appalachian Trail. My nerves were racked with fear and anxiety. Yet my assuredness was rock solid that I could complete this immense journey.

Chapter TWO

With butterflies in my stomach, the morning of March 26, 2013, I began the long drive south along Interstate 95, 85, and the backcountry roads to the southern terminus of the Appalachian Trail. The trail is near a small town, called Dahlonega, Georgia. My nerves were both excited and anxious at the same time.

It was early evening when I arrived, about a twenty-mile drive from Dahlonega, Georgia.

The hotel room I stayed in smelled of friction and Starbursts. My large backpack sat at the foot of the bed. Outside, a man was working raucously on his Ford Explorer. I laughed out loud to myself because I was having trouble sleeping, but now I was kind of pissed. In the middle of the night I went to the front desk and told the manager that I was checking out. She saw that I was annoyed and asked what the problem was. I explained, and she was apologetic.

As I was driving to the trailhead, the dashboard read 1:30. I realized I would be starting my trek along the Appalachian Trail as a night hiker. A night hike my first day out. What could go wrong?

"Hey watch this! Hold my water!" I thought to myself. The funny part being that I gave up beer. A popular expression before an accident goes more like, "Hey watch this! Hold my beer!"

When I opened my truck door at the trailhead, I was immediately hit in the face with bone-chilling cold gusts of wind that quite literally took my breath away. It was dark and eerie at the base of the dirt road where the AT crossed. I looked up at the sky and saw thinning clouds ripping through the night sky like jackrabbits running from a fox.

Although there was diversity, my body and mind were both comfortably seated on this journey.

As I approached the summit of Springer Mountain and the official southern terminus of the Appalachian Trail, I saw a few other hikers out with me, experiencing the snow flurries, high winds, ice on the trail, and a gloriously beautiful full moon to boot. I felt my three-hundred-pound-plus body telling me something. "GO!"

In the dark of the trail, my footsteps became my close companions. The light from my headlamp was bright enough to see where I was going, but at times, my toe would still hit a root or rock. Let me tell you, that shit hurts. So many more toe injuries would happen during this adventure. I learned to suck it up and keep on moving. "HUSS!" The trail zigged and zagged over the land. Trail maintainers were doing a bang-up job in Georgia to my observation. There were nice wooden bridges over the many streams, and even in the dark I found them to be comfortable to hike over. Of course sturdy and safe, two adjectives that would describe what any thru-hiker would want for a present.

The hidden treasures of the vagabond kind, moving along the dirt path, the first shelter I came to was the Stover Creek Shelter. The three-sided building and all the tent sites surrounding it were full.

Onward I walked toward Maine; somewhere around 2,180 miles left to hike, plus the steps to water, shelter, and towns . . . this adventure is around the 2,500-plus-mile variety. A little out of breath and tired, the next sign I came to read "Hawk Mountain Shelter." The sun was kissing the treetops when I arrived at the three-sided structure, and a few birds were chirping to indicate it was time to wake up. But for me, it was time for sleep.

There was movement from other travelers getting their water and preparing meals for the day's hiking plan. Inside, a tarp was set up to block the snow and chilling winds from the night before and there were two hammocks hung snuggly on the beams inside. I said my good mornings to many of the folks I saw. I then asked where the water was. I dropped my pack, changed from my hiking boots to my camp shoes (which were just sandals), and walked to the source of my hydration. It was a dangerous water getting as I almost slipped into the frigid waters more than once. I felt some soreness as I headed back to my things, but I felt very much alive, as well.

My shelter was a used, colorful, child-sized tent. The only way I could sleep comfortably was lying corner to corner. After I had set it up, I began receiving compliments on my beautifully handmade Hinkle Ukulele. The ukulele was white and the paint was still aromatic in its newness. I enjoyed her company and was happy that Larry and the Hinkle Ukulele Shop made her specifically for this adventure. She had two holes, one hole facing upward for my ears and one for the universe I tried to play her in. I did my best in making up songs as I went along. A guitarist not familiar with a ukulele would ask about notes and finger placement. I would give the simplest explanation and blow their mind.

"Have you ever played guitar with a capo on the fifth fret? Well, the bottom four strings are ukulele chords."

After that I would listen to better musicians than I play some pretty stellar songs, including, but not limited to, some Grateful Dead. No motor vehicles, horns, loud banging to hinder the close-knit community; a peaceful life cannot be measured. Music in the wilderness is a blessing.

Climbing into my tent, I clambered into my zero-degree sleeping bag. My girth would not allow me to zip it all the way up; to move around to get the best warmth was usually zipper side down on my sleeping pad. It did not take long for me to be sawing logs in the Georgia mountain sun.

I went to sleep at around nine a.m. and woke up to the sounds of pots clanking and the smell from the other hikers' lunch. It was around noon, and I woke up to also eat and communicate with my fellow foot travelers.

Other hikers were sitting around the picnic table. I did the same as I prepared my meal. Neil and Andy were from Connecticut, and both were attempting a thru-hike. Laura and Curtis were also out hiking together. A dad and daughter pair, they were very kind and super fun company. Greenlite was on the trail for a second attempt, trying to hike through to Maine. I didn't know proper trail etiquette regarding trail names, but I wanted one before I got one I didn't like. Curtis said, "Uke." I liked it, and it stuck. Maybe there was a discrepancy on who coined my trail name first, but I'm pretty sure it was Curtis. Laura would get her trail name later, Little Bird, and Curtis would take a blues brother persona along with him, Elwood. I gave Neil a trail name that would not stick once he found out that it was the name of Frank Zappa's daughter. He would have a trail name later on that would stick with him, called Yote. Andy remained Andy, but he was a great hiking partner. Then there was Rip from Texas. He got his trail name because he was climbing along a steep grade and ripped his hiking pants. A great bunch of people gathered around a picnic table unaware what the next several months would hold.

The conversation amongst hikers often came around to gear, a dreaded topic amongst ultra-light folks as opposed to people who brought whatever made them feel comfortable, ultra-heavy. I was ultra-heavy starting out, for sure. Carrying too much can hinder a thru-hike for some. Taking too little can also impede a thru-hike for others. But the mantra that flies strongly amongst the hiking community is HYOH or Hike Your Own Hike. It is important if you do not agree with someone's way of hiking that you let them do them, or they do they, or who dey? We dey!

As we all finished up our lunches and I began to pack up, there was someone in the shelter being loud and ornery. An elderly lady was speaking very negatively about life and it's unfortunate happenstances. She was going on about her family issues, issues with grandkids, and too much for my ears. I needed the positive uplift and not the other way around before I began hiking again. So I walked around to the back of the shelter, where Alpine Bomber, a girl from the same state I came from, Virginia, was a much-needed relief to me on the curve of negative versus positive. She was impressed that I was out there and exclaimed on more than one occasion that I would finish the AT journey. I appreciated that from her.

We both hiked out of the camp together, and when we reached the next forest road, she explained that she was staying there to wait for her mom, who was taking her back to Virginia. Bummer, as I thought she would be good trail company.

I made camp twice within a few miles. My body was adjusting and I needed to pace myself. I set up camp near Elwood and Little Bird at Horse Gap. The night was very windy, and I had difficulty setting up camp because of the high winds through the gap. Once I was settled into my sleeping bag, and my body heat warmed me, all was right with the world. Getting up the next morning was a daunting task. It was frigid outside. I wasn't sure of the temperature, but the wind chill was brutal. I rubbed my legs together to create friction for warmth. The movement was essential. Frostbite could set in. Once I hurriedly packed up my things, I noticed my hiking poles on the signpost heading up the mountain. I didn't know where I misplaced them, but Little Bird and Elwood put them there for me, a kindness I would come to appreciate when, on several occasions, I would have face-planted if I did not have them.

Once I packed up and hiked again, it only took about fifteen minutes for my body temperature to go from shivering to "I need to get out of this coat." Once I got moving, each mountain became easier than the next. I had a pattern as I climbed. I would count twenty-seven steps and then take a ten second, or longer, break. In one of the gaps, the army corps of engineers left a "water buffalo." It was a big tank of fresh water for the hikers. I thanked the absent person or persons for the gift. While I was there, I met a few other hikers whom I offered trail names. Some stuck and some changed along the way. I was all good with it. It was in fun, and I hope they enjoyed my company. Because I enjoyed their laughter at a big, silly guy hiking Georgia with a goal to walk to Maine. In their minds, I assume they thought I would give up. Maybe after telling them I gave up beer and was walking over two thousand miles to get one. This fact is funny and crazy, but believable.

The path to Gooch Mountain Shelter was pretty brutal. Being passed by other hikers is one thing, but some of them were moving at 3 miles per hour to my 1.5 miles per hour. As I was crossing a well-built and maintained wooden bridge, I heard a female voice from behind me, "Uke!" It was Alpine Bomber, and she decided to hike on instead of return to Virginia. Her pace was pretty incredible, and I did all I could to keep up, but told her I would meet up with her at the shelter. It was early evening when I finally arrived, but I didn't arrive. I had thought I was there, but I could not see or hear anyone. If it had not been for Alpine slacking back for me to make sure I was okay, I probably would have done camp a few hundred yards from the shelter and would not have even known it.

I got into the camp area of Gooch Mountain, settled into a cozy area of the refuge, and listened to Yote play the Hinklele. He was an excellent musician, and we were happy to have the distraction while we were preparing to do our evening rituals. Some folks were building a fire in the fire ring while I was cooking my dinner of red beans, rice, and a tuna packet. I sat eating when a guy from Florida, named Jake, and I started up a conversation. I explained that I was going to finish eating and head off to dreamland before the sunset so I could wake up early to night hike a bit. He expressed an interest in also hiking out with me at that time and asked if I could wake him up.

I was awake at one thirty as my head popped up on the second level of the Gooch Mountain Shelter where Jake was bedded down. When I shined my headlamp on him, he was eagerly looking at me. We quickly made breakfast, got our water, packed up, and hiked out. Jake and I had some medicine from mother earth as we hiked north. We smoked and I became euphoric. Then I realized I hadn't seen my truck keys and was afraid I may have lost them.

I stopped and began looking through my bag as a chilly wind blew and snow flurries fell around us. I found them the damn things, and we hiked on, laughing all the way.

My ukulele was stowed away on the sternum strap of my backpack. While I hiked, I would strum it, sometimes loudly. A few times when I thought a bear maybe in the vicinity, I would play my uke thunderously and yell, "Get outta here, bear!" Jake would reply to my bear deterrent by saying, "Ain't nobody got no time for that!" This phrase would be useful to many a hiker and repeated with laughter on many occasions. Go ahead, say it to yourself. It's fun. As we continued on Jake and I discussed his trail name. He was a fan of Emergency-C, a powdery substance that mixes with water and launches a thousand milligrams of Vitamin C to the head. So it was appropriate that Jake be named, Vita-C. And so it was.

We hiked past Gooch Gap and Copper Gap Road, where we took pictures of ourselves in the darkness with our headlamps. We passed Grassy Gap, Liss Gap, Jack's Gap, Tritt

Gap, and somewhere in the mess of gaps, we began our ascent of Big Cedar Mountain. It was not a high elevation gain, but I still used my twenty-seven-to-ten step ration to the halfway point, and I needed more than a ten-second break. As the sun canoodled with that Georgia sky that morning, it was if whatever deity was painting for us that day wanted us to know everything was going to be okay. The orange mixed with a dark blue, the lavender, and red. I needed time to enjoy what I was seeing, plus I was pretty tired. When we continued to the top of the mountain, we came to a huge rock that jettisoned out, forming a kind of table. I asked Vita-C if he wanted some coffee. I boiled some water in my cooking stove and had coffee on for our morning pick-me-up. Vita-C offered some snacks and some Emergen-C. We drank our black coffee while staring out at the expanse of the bare trees, a colorful skyline, and a spectacular open view of the Georgia's barren beauty.

It was getting late in the morning, and people were up and began to pass us heading up the mountain. I put my cooking stove away, and away we hiked. We arrived at Woody Gap parking area, where I needed to hitchhike to Suches for my resupply. I didn't think Vita-C would want to go all the way to town with me where I may hold him up, but he did, and I enjoyed his company. The parking lot was empty when we got our hitch into town. I had to wait for the post office to open, and that was enough time to charge our phones and other technology before hitchhiking back to the parking area.

The hitch was pretty quick and, of course, it would be in the back of a pickup truck. "Err yeah!" Our ride brought us back to the trailhead, and what did our eyes see? Trail magic![2] If you are not familiar with trail magic, it is where kind people bring love and support to places on the trail through foodstuff and often water. Water, more often than not, is the most exciting thing to see when hiking over several miles where there are little to no water sources. In this case, cheeseburgers, hotdogs, Gatorade, and brownies were a welcome sight. I just resupplied, and my pack weighed as much as a medium-sized toddler, but I was not complaining. Vita-C began gathering wood for a

---

[2] Individuals, friend groups, church groups, etc are often found along the trail, usually at road crossings, with goodies for hikers to consume. Trail Magic also comes from family and friends at the post office, sent general delivery to hikers. These goodies are made with love from complete strangers to familiar family and friends.

fire near where the trail magic folks were set up. I followed suit, and before too long we had a nice campfire.

Although the food was excellent, we needed to push on. Vita-C wanted to make Blood Mountain and the outfitters before they closed because he had his resupply box sent there. That would be another 10 ½ mile on top of the five we had already completed from Gooch Mountain Shelter. I hiked hard, but once I felt the hot spot under my foot, I knew I needed to stop. Vita-C stuck with me as I took off my boot and quickly painted the hot spot with super glue and applied the moleskin. Moleskin is used to prevent blisters or when hikers feel a warm spot beginning to rub their foot. Moleskin is good stuff, but it does not stick well. It was important for me to dry my foot, apply super-glue, and then the moleskin. I threw my boot back on, and away we hiked. I just could not make the summit of Blood Mountain this day. Vita-C and I hiked into Woods Hole Shelter and spent the night. A respectful 12 mile day for me.

We had the shelter to ourselves, except for a couple who pitched their tent about twenty yards away. The privy[3] (a.k.a. bathroom) was located past them another fifteen yards. I yelled out, "Iiiit's pooooopy doooopy time!" Vita-C laughed as he was already on his way before me. I would have to wait while he did his business first. Pooping outside in the wilderness must be a responsible endeavor. If there is not a privy in sight, it is important hikers dig a hole and poop in the hole, and then, of course, bury it well. He and I got settled in, set up our sleeping arrangements, and ate our dinner. Both of us were pretty tired. Not long after my head touched down, I was fast asleep.

We woke up to the sun and were ready to hike to the summit of Blood Mountain, Georgia. Vita-C hiked on ahead while I caught up with Andy, who was nursing a bum knee. He and I walked together for a while before I asked him if he was feeling okay. He said he was, and I hiked on up into the expanse of an amazing Georgia morning skyline with some cool people. Good people, as far as we all knew, who were all struggling with something weighing on our minds. It's amazing what a prescription of Nature will do to the most hardened folks.

---

[3] Privy- like old timey out houses, these wooden/concrete structures give hikers the relief they need without having to dig a hole to poop in somewhere off trail. Much respect goes to the volunteers who maintain and clean these aromatic wilderness bathrooms.

Reaching the summit of Blood Mountain, I received applause for my success from a very loving trail family[4]. The Blood Mountain summit crew included a woman from Tennessee, named Lost-n-Found, two funny British blokes, named Ali and Rich, Endian from Georgia, Alpine, Vita-C, Yote, and myself. So uplifting and inspiring was the experience, and I was only three days in and thirty miles down. I love and appreciate each one of the people who stood with me that day on the top of the huge rock shelf of Blood Mountain. There would be hundreds more mountains in in my life at that very moment. Someone gave me a congratulatory Snickers bar and many of us exchanged hugs. Fantastic, this trail life is. The warmth and understanding of our fellow human folks are very special.

The hike down from Blood Mountain was brutal on my knees. I decided to fall back and join Andy. His knee was not happy with him in the least either. The two of us met up with the rest of our Blood Mountain summit crew at the road crossing and outfitters.

As luck would have it, Lost-n-Found thought it would be a good idea to rent a cabin instead of staying at the hostel or hiking up the trail a ways and camping on the trail somewhere. A cabin meant showers, nice sleep, and warmth. A cabin in Georgia . . . life is what happens when we're busy making other plans, quite literally.

We were all smiles once we got settled. It just so happened that the Blood Mountain Cabin folks picked up all of our dirty laundry to clean. Then, they delivered it back. So clean smelling, so much appreciation for human people who care about other human people.

The hiker community was abuzz with talk of a shindig going down at the outfitter for hikers. There would be grub and good drink for any and all hikers wishing to attend. So that is what the seven of us did. The walk up to the outfitter from the cabins was a pain, but then again, the pain was everywhere in my body at this point. We made it to the party, where the food was delicious and the beer was forbidden, for me. I did

---

[4] Trail Family aka Tramily: Hiker strangers that become close friends in the weeks and months of rugged hiking.

spy an old Georgia head in the background of the party and knew I needed to make his acquaintance.

His name was Lumpy, and, yes, he did have some southern moonshine for my tasting pleasure, and, yes, it did take some canoodling on my part to get the goodness from his jar to my lips. He was a character of the highest order and funny as shit. We drank some shine and chatted about the trail community, the state of the union, and overall good, old-fashioned country talk. It was a breath of fresh air for me. I thanked Lumpy for his hospitality, but not before I called Vita-C and Yote over, as well, to taste the goodness of southern shine.

When we arrived back at the cabin, sleeping arrangements were made haphazardly of course. There was plenty of laughter and me annoying my comrades with talk in the middle of the night about water. Like a man in the desert searching for the hidden pool.

The next morning the groans and moans were prevalent, but it was important to get out early and hit the next milestone of however miles out or, more importantly, what my body was able to handle. Some grub and a picture of our group before we hiked on. As I was toward the tail end of the pack, I witnessed what drafting meant in hiking. Their pace up the hill was inspiring, but I was not going to keep up, I already knew that. I just kept my wits about me and rested when I needed to . . . and sometimes when I didn't.

Being passed shouldn't feel all that discouraging, but it did. Being passed and feeling the wind of the people passing me was disheartening, but I still kept moving forward. I rested when I needed, snacked when I needed, and drank plenty of water when I came to streams.

The sun was heading down fast when I hit the mountains before the descent into the Low Gap Shelter. These mountains should not have been that big of a deal, but it was like they never ended. I would complete one and then look up the next one with disgust. Growling and grunting, I moved my fat ass up that trail. I told myself, I said, "Self, you can—no—you *will* do this!" When I thought I was at the last mountain, I was sure of it, and then another popped up. Cursing my instincts, thinking I was closer than I was, I gurgled up some well-needed anger to push my ass up yet another mountain.

After I heaved and hoed the twenty-seven-to-ten step ratio up to the top, I looked down and to the right and was happy when I saw a flicker of fire.

"Marco!" Alpine yelled from below.

"Polo!" I mumbled down from above.

I hiked the switchbacks down into the camping area. Switchbacks are designed to make a trail more casual in the steepness of the grade. The problem is, these conveniences take more time to hike than if the trail would just jettison straight up the mountain. I got a little annoyed, but the surrounding visuals were enough to not complain too much about it.

I asked how long they all got there before me to gauge my speed and to be able to compare it for future hikes. It varied between fifteen and thirty minutes. My hiking speed would only increase as I continued my journey, I surmised. I went to say hello to Vita-C and asked him why he didn't save me a spot in the shelter. I knew he tried to, but it was an unaccepted practice for the hikers who hiked in before me. Damn did I wish there were room though.

"Sleep under the shelter," Vita-C advised.

"No way, man," I grunted.

"Suit yourself."

I was hangry[5] and tired, so I needed to find a place to sleep. Finding out the shelter was full, I scoped out somewhere to set up my colorful pup tent. There were a lot of people, more than I expected. So I ended up setting my tent up at the bottom of a ravine. I went down to the shelter where the water was, and I was thirsty. There was some loud talking by the water source. The opening of the building looked down to the water source, and I also noticed that many of the folks in the shelter were sitting up in

---

[5] Hungry + Angry = Hangry

their sleeping bags observing the interesting conversation happening at the watering hole. I walked over to the shelter folk and began doing a running commentary of what we all were viewing, calling it, "Shelter TV." Jerry Springer didn't have anything on what we were listening to. The laughter exploded at my commentary, and they caught me. The watering hole folks looked up at us and went silent. I will not go into detail about the conversation because these folks are my friends. And sometimes, what happens in the wilderness stays in the wilderness.

I got my water and headed back to my tent. A freeze-dried meal provided me with some needed energy. I hung out by the fire for a bit before settling in for the night. Again, once my head hit the tent floor, I was out in dreamland somewhere. I believe I was dreaming of orange juice, steak, crab cake sanniches, and other accouterments.

There was a pitter-patter that woke me up. Pitter- Patter- Pitter Patter -Pitter Patter. I thought, "Oh geez. This pup tent is going to be put to the test." The pitter-patter did not let up and became stronger before an all-out thunderstorm was stirring all around us. I felt my sleeping pad rise from the stream that was moving from underneath my circus pup tent. I frantically began packing my things into my backpack without regard to any order. I threw my boots on and started running my dry things to the shelter. There was a small area toward the back of the shelter that remained dry. I threw my pack down and ran back to my tent for the rest of my things. I was furious about what was happening, but all I could do was laugh. I laughed hard at this situation because my tent was more than wet inside. My ukulele was wet, but I saved her first and foremost. I left the tent and returned to my things. Then I crawled a bit under the shelter, where people were sleeping, as well. I was lucky to get the spot available. Once I got into my sleeping bag, I needed sleep if I was going to get up early and continue the hike north. Sleep I did.

The next morning I was woken up by "the Germans," who it was said took a bunch of the trail magic water and left little for everyone else. I met other German people later on who were nothing like these two jagoffs. People of all different varieties hike the long trails of America each year; each has hers or his characteristics that go well with, or demean, the trail. It can be argued that the Germans from Low Gap who took the brunt of the water knew little English and perhaps did not know any better. That is my hope. Otherwise, yes, they're jagoffs.

My body was yelling at me when I stood up. From my dirt bed, I recalled the events of the previous night. It wasn't like it just sprinkled a little bit; the rains came down in sheets. I was lucky to get my sleeping bag out in time. Down and water just don't mix. I stretched as much as possible before getting into my camp shoes and moving to the campsite. I was afraid to walk to my tent and see what the major storm did to it. Luckily the sun was creeping in for some positive uplift and drying my wet things.

I walked up to see my tent upended by the wind and rain. On its side, my tent looked like a sore sight. Some people were already hiking out on the trail when I started taking my tent down. I heard some snide comments and laughter about my experience, but I waved them off and continued to think, *Rainbows and unicorns . . . rainbows and unicorns . . . ukulele song . . . rainbows and unicorns.*

I took my tent down to the rest of my things by the shelter. Vita-C's words from the previous night rang in my ear, "You can sleep under the shelter." If I had listened to his advice, I would have been dry and ready to hike out. As it turned out, it took me several hours before I was ready to hike on. My top string in my pack went into the hole, and I was having trouble getting it out to cinch up my sack. "Ha ha ha," I said. "Cinch up my sack." Luckily that is when I met Honey Badger and Kowabunga. The two hiked into Low Gap together. Kowabunga said he was from Pennsylvania and Honey Badger said she was from Virginia. The two had met on the trail, but were kicking up dust. I would find that these two were very fast hikers.

Kowabunga wanted me to play my ukulele. I obliged, and he recorded something funny I sang on his phone. I asked Honey Badger if she could retrieve my string so I could cinch up my sack. She accepted the challenge and quickly recovered it from inside the string holder. I played a few more strums on the ukulele and began the dreaded pack up and go. It was April 1st, but I was not aware of that when I left them during the late morning. My legs were feeling stronger, and I pushed hard to make about two miles an hour. I even passed a few folks, which shouldn't be a big deal, but when you had as been slow as I had, there was a little guilty pleasure in it.

Honey Badger and Kowabunga caught up to me a few hours later and hiked quickly past me. The trail had some slippery rocks and a long way down on one side and a steep uphill on the other side. The two of them were about thirty yards ahead when I heard Honey Badger, "Uke! Hurry, Kowabunga fell! Come quick! He hurt his ankle!" It was a sight to see my fat ass running at top speed over the rugged terrain. They took a picture to memorialize the event. I ran up to them, and I saw a glint in Honey Badger's eyes. I'd been, had! "April Fools!" they both yelled out. We all smiled and laughed a bit, of course at my expense. I was good at it; I like a good laugh, especially at my expense.

That energy in running those thirty yards I would want back later when I climbed into the Blue Mountain Shelter. It took a bunch of gumption to work my legs over the rock fields and up the many rock steps leading up to the water source just before the shelter. I was able to camel up a bit and snag some water for my dinner later on before walking the next twenty yards up to the camping area.

Around the campfire, I ate my dinner and enjoyed many good folks laughing and enjoying life at the moment. It was time for an early bedtime to be up again bright and early for another grueling day. I apologized to my trail friends in advance again for being noisy in the early morning. I slept well until I heard a girl scream. I understood that a mouse had walked over her sleeping bag, and she swatted up in the air, and it landed on someone else. It was somewhat of frenzy, but the shelter calmed down, and I was able to fall quickly back asleep.

Two a.m. came, and I was starting my water to boil for my homemade oatmeal. A ziplock bag filled with plain oatmeal, a bit of sugar, a dash of nutmeg, a dash of cin-namon, cran-raisins, raisins, and walnuts. As it cooked, the smells wafted throughout the shelter. I then made a Carnation instant breakfast. After I had washed up from breakfast, I hiked out and grabbed some water before leaving the area.

It was a crisp spring morning walk. The descent was approximately 1,076 feet into Unicoi Gap, which, of course, I kept calling it "Unicorn Gap" because you can be yourself, but if you can be a unicorn, well . . . be a unicorn. The road was quiet as I continued across Highway 17. Throughout the day, hikers were flying by me. Except the folks who hitched into Helen, Georgia, but it was a productive hiking day. Then a rise and fall over

Rocky Mountain and into Indian Grave Gap. Getting to the top of Tray Mountain was a twenty-seven/ten huff and puff of almost a thousand feet. Down the other side, I broke for lunch at Tray Mountain Shelter. Endian hooked me up with one of his noodle meals. I threw a tuna packet in for some much needed protein. After lunch, I enjoyed some more rest and good company with Endian in the fresh Georgia mountain air. It had one incredible vista to boot. When I began hiking again, I felt recharged, hiking firm into Sassafras Campground, where Lost-n-found, her English chums Ali and Rich, Happy Feet, and her friend were already set up and building a fire. I asked if it was okay if I camped with them, and they said it was alright. Then I asked where I could find the water source. They explained it was a good hike down the hill, and they were not wrong. I had already put on my camp shoes and headed down the steep descent to the source of my hydration.

I got to the water as the sun was not cooperating with my schedule. As my mind was racing around this fact, my right foot slipped into the frigid water. Luckily I did not change into my camp socks before going to get my water, or I would have either had to put on a dirty pair or the pair I just hiked in that day. I would have opted for the dirty pair, but luckily . . . luckily. I climbed out of the water source, and my breathing was heavy when I finally reached camp. The routine was becoming a little bit more tolerable each day I was out, but my aching body was screaming at me as I crept into my sleeping bag. I noticed that I was able to zip my bag up a little farther, a good sign that my body was changing physically.

During the night, I was startled awake by what sounded like two hundred screaming babies: coyotes, only about thirty or so yards away. Apparently, they were making a fresh kill of prey. They were happy, and although they kept me awake for the next thirty minutes or so, I was very glad that I and my camping companions were not their snacks.

I was the last one out of camp because everyone was racing into the next trail town of Hiawassee, Georgia. Once I got myself together, I tried to kick it into gear, but there was this little mountain that had an elevation of over nine hundred feet in less than a mile. That was a big deal for my body. I took several breaks between my twenty-seven steps and much over ten-second stops. Once I crested to the top of Kelly Knob, I felt a bit dizzy, but kept my composure when I saw two hikers making the peak at the same point as me. For some unknown and very annoying reason, my mind always went to ask people I saw two questions: How far something was? And how the water source was? As I continued this greenhorn adventure, I realized that I did not have to ask this as much. I still asked at times when my body was not feeling up to snuff for that day's activities.

There was some trail magic when I hit the road to Hiawassee, Georgia. I was happy to be there on April 3rd, my seventh day on the trail and seventy miles conquered. Seventy miles a week without a day off—I was happy with it because I knew that with time, I was going to break that mileage several times over the course of the next six and a half months.

Within five minutes I was able to thumb a ride to town to rest in a motel room with my trail friends. Kowabunga, Rip, a nice woman from Georgia, named Moose, Andy, Low Rider, and I sat at an all-you-can-eat buffet. We gorged ourselves on things like roast beast, chicken, veggies, mac and cheese, mashed potatoes, and a big healthy salad with all the trimmings. I ordered an orange juice, even though it was dinnertime. When I tasted the liquid on my lips, it was weirdly joyful. My body was changing with each and every Appalachian Trail step I took. The appreciation for things like orange juice, a good meal, and the kindness of others was a happy feeling.

After dinner, we walked over to Endian's hotel room at the Holiday Inn. Myself, Endian, Vita-C, Honey Badger, and Kowabunga all enjoyed, overly enjoyed, the hotel hot tub. Many a hiker soaked their weary bodies in that hot heavenly goodness. Once we got out, I could already feel my muscles loosening up. It felt exquisite, and I thanked Endian for his generosity.

Once Kowabunga, Honey Badger, and I returned to our motel, there was a good campfire and about twenty or more hikers all gathered round it, setting off a beautiful night of wild debauchery. The three of us, including Endian, already decided that we were hiking out the next morning. So we declined several invitations to join in the fun.

Later we heard that Greenlite had fallen into the fire. He was not a big hiker but, Rip, the hiker closest to him, was a large man like me. He picked him straight out of the fire and began smacking the hot coals from his burned and tattered shirt. Luckily that Rip had been in the right place at the right time to save him from getting too badly burned.

Before heading to bed, Kowabunga helped me with a pack breakdown because I was still a bit ultra-heavy. I think we managed to eliminate a pound or two from my pack weight, for which I thanked him and prepared for a restful night's sleep before the four of us would be hiking out early the next morning.

The next morning we woke up with pep in our step and the whispers of rain on the horizon for our day's hike back out into the Georgia wilderness, which just so happened to be our last steps on this journey in the peach state.

Chapter THREE

I sat on the edge of the bed staring down at my pack and some things I still had not managed to stuff into it. Learning how to pack a long distance backpack takes time, practice, and overall experience. Some packs have a zipper at the bottom to make sleeping bags more accessible. I used a contractor's garbage bag inside as a liner from the rain, so this zipper was pretty much useless. My loose sleeping bag first, then my cooking stove, and on top of that I had my dry camp clothes, which consisted of a dry pair of socks, cold weather liners of a shirt and pant, running shorts, and a cotton T-shirt. My food bag went on top of my dry clothes. Then toward the top of the pack were accessible items like a rain jacket and a baggy of snacks for the short breaks. The other pockets around my pack held my phone, camera, first-aid stuff, my knife, and a small stuffed guardian angel my friend, Mollie, had given me before I left.

I looked down at my pack, watching my company prepare a little faster, and someone was yelling out, "The van is going to be here in five minutes!" or something to that effect. I was shoving the remainder of my belongings into my pack. I put on my boots, left the hotel room, and yelled out to all my hung-over hiking community good-byes along with a loud song. Probably "Here Comes the Sun" or "Zip-a-Dee-Doo-Dah." Later I would get some glares from them for the abrupt and annoying wake-up. They got the last laugh, though, as the day would be forever termed, "hell day" and for good reason.

Several hikers headed out to the trail, got into the van. Our driver took us to the trail-head and dropped us off at the beginning of a light rain. Once we got out, we all immediately grabbed for our raincoats and packed covers to keep our stuff somewhat dry, fingers crossed.

Kowabunga, Endian, Honey Badger, and Vita-C started out at a nice, fast pace. I trudged my big happy ass along without wearing myself out too quickly. Vita-C fell back with me and helped me keep somewhat of an even pace. He helped me a great deal on my initial greenhorn hike that would inevitably turn me into a much more efficient hiker. You know, for the end of days.

The breeze turned into stronger winds as we steadily climbed the mountain. The smell of earth and decay filled our nostrils as the rain continued its back and forth from a light mist to a heavy spray. Vita-C was a great friend to me on the trail, but I could tell I was holding him up. I explained to him that it probably was not helping him keeping my pace and said just to go ahead without me. I would make it to camp and see him when I arrived. He was reluctant but agreed that we would see each other at camp.

Hiking alone can be very lonely at times, but other times it's just what one needs to free some cobwebs of thought from an ever-racing brain. Thoughts like "What the hell am I doing out here in the rain, in the middle of the forest, without a clue what my next step will hold?" Also, thoughts of my childhood would run through my lizard brain and what it meant to grow up in a small community of humans.

When my father used to pick my sisters and me up for weekends after his and my mom's divorce, we would often stop at my Aunt Leona and Uncle Duane's in North Creek (outside of Emporium). On one particular summer weekend, we stayed to hang out. I think I may have been around six or seven years old at the time. It was a beautiful day in Pennsylvania, and one of my cousins had the idea to go to the creek and catch crawfish or something of that nature.

My cousins, two sisters, and I all went down to the stream to cross it. My cousin, Duane, crossed first, followed by my cousin, Shawn, my other cousin Renee, my sister, Tonya, and then my sister, Teresa. I followed behind Teresa and looked down at the clear, calm stream. I could see the earthy colored rocks between ripples of water going by my bare feet. When I reached the middle of the stream, I noticed a muddy color replace the neutral color I was just seeing. And then I felt a jolt of rushing water, and down the stream I went. Teresa screamed out and also fell in the quickening water behind me. A flash flood was not in the plan, but when are they really? About fifteen yards away, an enormous felled oak tree stopped both of us from more than likely drowning, or at the very least a hospital visit.

As Teresa and I hung on a huge tree trunk for dear life, I saw my cousin, Duane; jumped out onto the great span of the tree and grab both of my hands, dragging my sopping wet butt out and over the trunk like a rug over a banister. Then he stepped over to Teresa and repeated the same. Teresa and I gingerly crawled to safety on the bank of the now-rushing torrents being poured down into the valley. We walked back to the house, soaking wet, my father not at all pleased, but happy we were all safe.

The sign for the next and last Georgia shelter was in front of me as I snapped out of this blast from the past. It was a walk on a side trail from the Appalachian Trail to the Plum Orchard Gap Shelter. I stood there for a few minutes, wondering if I needed any water or an extended break. I was good on water, and I figured Vita-C and everyone else continued, so I did, as well. I had energy, and I felt good when I continued the upward momentum into North Carolina. Can ya hear me, North Carolina?

The rain continued to fall, mainly a mist when I hit the border and my last few steps of Georgia. I noticed to my left a young boy about the age of twelve in jeans and a T-shirt hunched under a rock ledge about ten yards from the trail. I asked him if he was okay, and he said he was. He explained that he was waiting on his mum. I asked him if he would mind snapping a picture of me by the North Carolina/Georgia sign. He did not mind and took a pretty cool shot.

He bounded down off of some rocks, and I then noticed he had a dog with him. He hollered at me as the dog trotted toward me, "He's nice!"

"Thanks," I said as I began to pet the German Shepherd.

I asked him if he wanted to hike ahead with me. I knew him sitting in the cold rain in blue jeans was not the best scenario for him, but he said his mum would be right along. I offered good luck, and he smiled and said the same.

I felt somewhat guilty as I walked away, but I could not be responsible for the lad. His mom would be there, and they would hike, hopefully back down the mountain to the dry and warmth of their car.

The rain let up some as I crested a hill. The trail veered off to the right. As I made the turn to the right, the fog began pouring in from the left side of the trail. In the distance, I could see an incredible sight. A gnarly tree, huge, branches like spindly arms waving in multiple directions. With the fog rolling in around it, it was magnificent. I was not going to stop, but I knew if I did not get this picture, I probably would kick myself later. Especially since the rain had just let up some. I dropped my pack, searched for my camera, and snapped a pretty great shot of the majestic oak tree. Dubbed the "sitting tree" by someone from trail lore past, it was a sight to behold. Pictures, again, never do something like that experience any justice.

I vacated the storied tree; the forest became an eerie place. I walked ahead and came to some stairs. As the trail wound around the mountain like Grinch's lair, the fog continued . . . until the sky opened up with a rain, hail, and sleet mixture from the depths of Hades. I began a light jog when I heard familiar voices behind me, yelling but sounding almost inaudible with the powerful storm raging around us.

Kowabunga and Honey Badger were yelling and running in the hail. As I looked back, I saw the boy from the border trailing behind them both. Leave it to Honey Badger to convince him to come along, dog in tow.

I asked them how I had got out in front of their jackrabbit selves, and they said they had stopped at the last shelter. I told them I continued because I did not want to get too far behind them. I was happy they were still near me and not miles ahead and that I was beginning to keep a better pace.

The sky was getting darker with each step toward the summit of Muskrat Creek. I knew I was not far away from it, but I was feeling fatigued. I heard voices before I arrived and trotted into another jog. The shelter was full and some jagoff had set his tent up inside the shelter, which cuts down on how many people can sleep in it. I heard Honey Badger and Vita-C yell, "Uke!"

Honey Badger, Endian, and Vita-C were lying on the earthen ground just outside the shelter but under the shelter's canopy. Some shelters on the AT had tall canopies, where many of the shelters were very basic with three walls and a floor. As I stood there talking with them, a guy from Georgia was standing in full rain gear with a piece of the awning. He introduced himself as Chris from Macon and explained that he would be hiking on into the storm. I asked him if that was a good idea, but he said he would be okay. Chris hung out for a while longer, chatting and getting some needed respite. I saw him put on the rest of his gear. He said his good-byes and we wished him safe travels.

There was a space between Endian and Vita-C with Honey Badger at their heads lying horizontally. I lay my tarp down in the space provided to me from my trail buds. Then I brought out my sleeping bag. I took off my wet clothes and hung them to dry. "Dry" is a relative term. I hung them to drip. I crawled into my sleeping bag and took off the remainder of my clothes. As I lay naked in my sleeping bag, I could feel my body heat warming me within the zero-degree sleeping bag. I boiled some water and made a dinner of fettuccini Alfredo and made some flavored water for my hydration for the following day. Once I finished my meal, I popped a few ibuprofens and sunk deep into my shell. I was able almost to zip my sleeping bag the entire way up.

My eyes popped open. My bladder was yelling at me, and there was no time to think. I began crawling out of me sleeping bag, but I had trouble getting my zipper undone as, unlike previous times, I was able to get the zipper all the way up, but my girth moved around in a way that my hands were not near the zipper. I struggled with the bag and became flustered when I settled back into the sleeping bag; I took a deep breath to calm myself and my aching bladder. A little finesse and banana pumpkins, the zipper moved, and I was out of my straightjacket. I stood up, put on my camp shoes, and headed to a tree outside of the camping area. The crisp, frigid air stung my naked body as the bright moon danced on my white skin, but relief came.

I sauntered quickly back to my warm home within my sleeping bag, but when I got in, it was cold. I needed to zip back up and wait to get warm again. I did a friction trick with my legs by rubbing them together in an almost runner style to make the heat come faster. Within minutes, I was back to dreaming about an eagle who was chasing me through a wooded forest and some other dreamy gems that kept me on my sleepy toes.

The voices were happy and loud the next morning. I rolled over and unzipped my sleeping bag after struggling with the zipper. I put on my shorts, stood up, and gave a guttural yawn. My body ached a bit, but for the most part, I felt good.

My thoughts were of hiking a good distance when I was beginning to pack, though I noticed that my sleeping bag was very wet. I set it to the side, prepared my breakfast, ate, and packed everything in my backpack, sleeping bag last.

The sky was clear when I hiked out alone. The rest of the crew got an early start, but I knew I would see them again. I had walked a few miles before I saw Chris in his bivy[6] sac behind a log. In my head, I thought how uncomfortable that would have been, but I saw him stick his head out and wave, so at least his spirits were in it.

The sun was coming up, and it felt warm and welcoming. I knew I needed to get my sleeping bag dry in case of colder temperatures during the night. The trail came to a cross of another trail system, but the white blaze was clearly marked. Along the Appalachian Trail there are white painted rectangular markings on trees, rocks, bridges, downed tree trunks, and other objects. These markings are used to assure hikers that the trail they're on is in fact the right one. I had walked about twenty-five yards before I saw the shelter to my right.

---

[6] Bivy- Or bivouac sack (also known as a, bivvy, or bivi) is an extremely small, lightweight, waterproof shelter, and an alternative to traditional tent systems. It is used by climbers, mountaineers, hikers, ultra light backpackers, soldiers and minimalist campers.

Standing Indian Shelter was empty when I arrived. I set my backpack down and immediately threw my sleeping bag up in the sun's rays to dry. I also set my tarp out to dry,
but I was not worried about that as much. I retrieved some water from the stream
below the shelter and began boiling some water for coffee.

I sat listening to the birds and the skittering around of some rodents. I walked around
the area, and I noticed a tent set up in the back. It was a beautiful tent, so I figured
some hikers decided to sleep in, so I didn't yell out to them or anything. Deep down I
didn't want to find a dead body. Why that goes through my head, who knows? But as
the hours passed and there was still no movement from the tent, my initial suspicion
of the hiker/s just sleeping was laid to rest. Either no one was in there or a corpse was
in there. I felt sorry that I didn't check when first arriving, but being that several hours
had passed, there was no way I was opening, hopefully, an abandoned tent.

I heard some voices at the front of the shelter and saw someone looking in my direction. They asked if that tent was mine and I explained that it was not, that I was just
drying my things. One of the hikers came back around to the tent and started shouting
and asking whoever was in there if they were all right.

Nervous chills went up my spine as there was no response. I walked back around to
the front of the shelter as they still were shouting for someone to respond. No way
did I want to see what my brain was telling me was in there.

"Nope, no one is in there. Someone just left a perfectly good tent up. Weird, maybe the
storm forced them to hike on?" A Hiker yelled out. I was relieved.

As I prepared my lunch, I decided to sleep during the daytime and hike out during the
night. I was comfortable with it, and it felt more my style, I suppose. More people began
to arrive at the shelter. Bonsai, whom I first met at Blue Mountain Shelter, Patchouli, a
kind woman from Wisconsin, First Gear and her cousin who were from Vermont, and
a few other hikers arrived sporadically throughout the afternoon and evening.

Before I went off into my daytime sleep, I explained to my hiking friends that I snore
when I am on my back—not when I am on my side, only to be woken up by loud fits

of laughter while the sun was casting the last bits of light on the camp. Of course, I asked what they were all laughing about, and someone said, "We thought you only snored while you were on your back." I guess I was breathing heavily while on my side too. Only when I am on my back, and not when I am on my side. They laughed about the randomness and went back to their conversations before my winded interruption.

I got up to take care of some poopy doopy time business and returned to a jubilant group. Patchouli and I were talking about my looming night hike. She showed an interest in joining me, and I happily agreed to have her as my hiking partner if she was willing to wake up in the middle of the night.

She decided to wake up. She and I would hike out between two a.m. and three a.m. the following morning. I got a restful night's sleep and hoped she had, as well, when I rose from my warm cocoon. She was already awake when I started my hot chocolate oatmeal concoction. The smell of chocolate permeated throughout the shelter, and I offered Patchouli some of it. She tried it, and I knew after her first bite that she'd want another one.

With packs donned, we headed out into a cloudless night. The moon lit up Standing Indian Mountain in the close distance. The winds were medium, but the chill was piercing. The movement was necessary for the cold of the night to accelerate the heart and add some body heat to the exploit. The stars were like headlights in the expanse of the North Carolina sky. Without artificial lighting, the world does seem a little more peaceful—eerie at times, as well, but mostly quiet.

As we zigzagged the switchbacks of Standing Indian Mountain, Patchouli was not feeling well within the first grueling uphill mile. We stopped to rest several times, and I was worried about her. I explained to her that it was important that we keep moving so we did not further the danger of both of our healths in the chill of the night air.

Before we crested the top of the mountain, I suggested we take one of our tents out to rest until she felt better to hike on. She agreed and apologized to me about the setback. When we found a suitable clearing, and I set up my pup tent, we both retrieved our sleeping bags. Once we were comfortable inside, I asked her if she was feeling better. She said she was not, but that the rest should help her. I was hopeful that that was the case. Sleep soon rushed over me, and REM was emerging. The dream I believe was of rainbows and unicorns. I think I was riding a unicorn! Yes! Well, that is what I think I remember dreaming. I cannot confirm or deny it.

I was groggy when I awoke from my very peaceful slumber only to turn over and see that Patchouli was not there. I was concerned until I unzipped my tent to find a very kind note from her. She did not sleep due to my snoring. I felt sorry but I was happy she felt better and was able to hike on.

It only took me a few minutes to pack back up and head up the trail. The morning sun was canoodling my face as I walked along the ridges before Albert Mountain. A milestone of having hiked one hundred miles in less than eleven days was a big deal to the people who were rooting for me from the sidelines of my craziness and for me.

Each day my body was feeling more and more into . . . something . . . a machine. I was becoming a well-oiled machine, replete with the strongest and loudest farts known to man. I found myself asking, "If a man farts in the woods and no one smells it but himself, does it still get a rating?" I could only attest to my flatulence . . . "A seven."

About a quarter of a mile before Albert Mountain, I was rather exhausted. The rocks were angry, and had it not been for my trekking pole, I am sure I would have fallen off the cliffside below. To the right of the trail was a precipitous drop. A rocky cliff was to my right, and as I hiked forward, my foot caught a root that grew into one of the rock steps. I lurched forward quickly, moving my right hand and hiking pole out in front of me. I just caught the edge of the cliff as every muscle in my upper body tensed, saving my life. Before righting myself, my head was several feet over the edge of the cliff, looking down at what would have been a rescue or a retrieval of my body. Whew to the muthafuckin' whew!

After a twenty-yard grueling scramble to the fire tower and the summit of Albert Mountain, I found liquid in my eyes. There were other folks up there, and I ducked away for a few minutes to compose myself before I went to say hello. No one I knew from the trail. I walked to the edge to an impressive view of the wild forest expanding the horizon out in front of me. I ate a snack and asked a day hiker if he would mind snapping a picture of me for my friends and family.

Euphoria engulfed me as I stepped into the next one hundred miles of my Appalachian Trail experience. There were many moments when I asked myself what the hell I was doing, and some of my friends were asking the same thing (some enemies more than likely, as well). But in that moment, like so many other moments, I knew I was going to make it to Maine. "Hell or high water" as the saying goes.

Chapter FOUR

Long Branch shelter was North Carolina's newest addition to their Appalachian Trail résumé, and damn if they did not nail it! No pun intended. I hiked sixteen miles to the side trail leading into the new shelter. This two-story, three-sided trail mansion was bursting with newness. In the air was the smell of freshly cut pine, and an excellent campfire that rose up in the afternoon was just what I needed. I could have hiked another eight or ten miles, but the atmosphere was too grand a style to leave it where I was seeing it. Living in the moment like a boss.

First Gear and her cousin, who I thought was her boyfriend since meeting them, came into camp, as well. A few other weary travelers, including a trail legend, were enjoying trail talk and good company. First Gear and I got the first spaces on the second floor of the taj-ma-shelter. Her smile can warm a bowl of Campbell's soup, lemme tell ya!

We bedded down and I again slept like a little fat ass baby (which I am sure many of my friends and non-friends alike have called me). I get it; I accept it. Owning our crazy lives is the most empowering way to be. With the whole beer thing, sure I was ornery with folks when I saw them drinking some of the top-of-the-line nectars like anything from Devils Backbone Brewery, Fat Tire, New Castle Brown Ale, any IPA, and a juggernaut of other high-quality heaven-in-a-bottle goodnesses. Wouldn't a crack addict watching someone smoke crack in front of them be on edge, as well? Okay, wrong analogy. But seriously, here and now, I apologize to anyone whom I may have offended with my whining about the beer they were drinking. Not to worry, though, I would have my beer soon enough.

It was somewhat difficult to leave the tranquility of the new wilderness oasis in the mountains, but it had to be done. A quick breakfast, privy poopy doopy time, and water getting led me again to donning pack and heading back on the rugged trail. A fly on the wall of the blue ball called Earth. Listening, watching, and observing the changes in the land like some lab tech with eyes under a microscope.

My pack felt somewhat lighter as my food storage was dropping. My sights were set on Franklin, North Carolina, where I would get a good night's sleep and a resupply from the post office. As my feet were hitting the trail, my eyes were hitting a gorgeous folding of mountains to my left along the many ridgelines. It doesn't matter; all of life's dramas swim out the window of a home underwater, caused by a great flood. It does not matter the opinions of others, even if those opinions happen to be spot on. It does not matter because in order for it to matter, we all need to accept that there is a problem. Like a drunk who doesn't accept that "just one" will more than likely be "just twenty."

Many trees were felled by what looked like a tornado that ran across the side of the mountain. I had to climb over more trees than I could count. I almost fell several times, but I kept my balance moving north. The sun was warm and I stopped to remove layers to keep my body heat down, as I would change more times than I would remember over the course of the next six and a half months.

Childhood memories of growing up in north central Pennsylvania would flood my memories, and I would remember things I thought I had forgotten. Like the time I first stole bubble gum when I was six. It was a favorite restaurant, called Luigi's. I was about four feet high and the owner, Joe DiBello, did not see me enter his establishment. I crawled behind the counter, grabbed a few pieces of bubble gum, and crawled to a doggy door that led to a refrigerator.

The large refrigerator door had another smaller door, like a doggy door, that I crawled through. I sat and ate the bubble gum, looking around at Italian ingredients for pizzas, famous Luigi's hoagie sauces, Italian meats, and different cheeses. Then I became bored sitting in the cooler, and I also felt cold. I went back to the small door and it would not open. Panic rose in my small body and I began knocking on the door. I then saw Joe's broad, black-bearded face shown in the window above me and scared the living shit out of me. He opened the cooler door and I ran past him. I could see the shock on his face, as well, when I ran to the door and down the front steps toward my grandmother's house on the corner of West Vine and West Fifth Streets in Emporium. There had been a search for me, and when I arrived, I tried to hide, knowing I was going to be in trouble. I saw my mother first, and to say she was angry would be an understatement. Furious was more like it, but maybe I saw a glint of relief, as well. But more anger than anything—she had that Italian temper that I became familiar with on more than one occasion. It would not be the last time I would make myself scarce throughout my life.

A quick stop for a snack and some ukulele playing in the Rock Gap Shelter and I was ready for town. The relaxing seven miles brought me to US 64, where I stood with my thumb out, waiting for a ride into the town of Franklin. It took less than ten minutes for a short ride into town by a father and son.

"Are you hiking the AT?" The kind gentleman asked me

"Yes, Sir." I replied

"That is awesome!" He exclaimed.

"Thanks. I think so, too."

After they dropped me off at a local gas station I walked to the motel and saw Patchouli and Bonsai hanging out. We all shared a room and ordered some food. I was sending some emails to friends and family who wanted to keep up with my adventures and did so at the motel office. I called it Bloyderlog. Looking back on that name, I realized it was awesome! I wish it would have worked better. Later my cousin Christopher would set up an awesome blog site for me called hikingtobeer.com. Grammar wasn't so much a thing as I just flew off with whatever was on my mind. Kind of like this book, here.

Patchouli and Bonsai went to town to run errands, and I did some needed laundering of some pretty grimy dirty clothes. The spring day in Franklin was welcome, except the part with the shrill of noise pollution in the city. More people should ride their bikes and walk. It just is better for you and for Earth. This is your public service announcement. Stop polluting the fragile landscape, assholes!

Later on in the evening, I met up with my old pals, Vita-C, Endian, and Honey Badger, and we hugged and laughed and sung and we tiptoed through the tulips. Okay, that last part we didn't do, but it was uplifting and positive to see them. No drama, just good people living.

Vita-C played my ukulele, aka, White Blaze for a little while, even though she was showing signs of wear and I was having some issues keeping her in tune. I am not a tune-by-ear type of guy, so without a tuner, it's one-string plucking, maybe two.

*Bed: a piece of furniture for sleep or rest, typically a framework with a mattress and coverings. For a thru-hiker, a bed is more than that. A bed is a cloud, something so many people in this spherical land take for granted, as with many other objects of their affections.

Patchouli, Bonsai, and I had a restful night's sleep. The next morning, a large group of us went to the local Franklin church for a homemade breakfast, a feast of pancakes, bacon, scrambled eggs, and orange juice. It was delicious. Once we were finished, we said our good-byes with appreciation. We headed back to the hotel and prepared for the day's adventure.

My hiking day would be short-lived. I hiked out with Som'Peach along a service road. We came to the trail, and I realized that I had missed some of it. I was a purist and somewhat of a jagoff when it came to hitting every part of the trail. Som'Peach laughed at me but indulged me by heading back to where I got off the trail the day before. He snapped a picture of me and away we went up a pretty steep incline, called the

Winding Stair Gap. It was rough for me, and I could not keep up with Som'Peach as I saw him streamline up the mountainside. I did my counting . . . twenty-seven steps . . . ten second break . . . no, two minutes . . . nope, let me just lie down a minute.

I was not happy with myself, but maybe the pancakes were weighing me down. I continued my hike until I reached an open field at the top of Silar Bald summit less than four miles north of Franklin. It was beautiful and a path jetted from the AT up to the top of the summit of the bald. I decided to make camp. I set up my tent and had a little snack before going up to the top of the bald. It was gorgeous, those southbound Georgia rolls and the westbound Tennessee stills. I could taste the whiskey in the air.

The sun began to set as I finished my supper of some tuna wraps and some flavored water. I bedded down to the sounds of high winds hitting the side of the tent. Being in the open has its perks, but when the forest surrounds the camp, the elements are not as harsh. Waking up the next morning was interesting because the wind would not allow me to fold my tent up correctly and my tarp was caught by a high wind and kited into a nearby thicket. I ran to get it, but not before it had some punctures in it from the sharp tree branches. I yelled some expletives but continued to pack up.

Once I was hiking again, I could feel a good day of hiking ahead. The bald was only less than a hundred feet before I hit the edge of the wood-lined forest. As soon as I walked into the forest, the high winds I was experiencing vanished. Stillness permeated not only my mind but my surroundings as I slid down the Appalachian Trail's ridgeline. The sound of birds chirping was a good sign, for spring was popping up all around me. It would not be long before I would begin to see the wildflowers, foraging forest creatures, and budding of the trees throughout the vastness of information I was taking in.

A twelve-mile day and I was comfortable with my routine: water getting, food prep, if time allowed I would most certainly build a fire, and bed. Trail lives are dependent on the weather, knowing that what we control is the ability to stay on a schedule and try our best to get as many miles completed throughout each passing day.

I was only a few miles from the NOC, or Nantahala Outdoor Center. Right before the long and very steep descent into the tiny village, there was an incredible view of the

Great Smoky Mountains from a ledge, called Jump-up Look Out. I quickly snapped a photo before climbing down a rock scramble to a more manageable trail. My toes would catch some roots on my way down, and it would hurt. My eyes would fill with tears a little, but I would swallow hard the pain.

The trail swerved in and out of the mountains folds, and I heard quickening footsteps behind me. A fellow thru-hiker moved pretty fast and passed me and jetted down the mountain toward town. I didn't even attempt to keep up. I let her pass and watched her incredible hiking gait as she descended into the switchbacks. Her trail name was Acorn, and I admired her. She also hiked from Georgia, and I figured with the pace she was moving at, I would not see her too many more times along this journey.

Once the trail dips into the last shelter before the road into town, the trail goes back up about a hundred feet. I hit the small climb; my knees, ankles, and overall body felt like pudding, sore, worn-out muscle pudding. The trail then made a turn, and I could hear the rushing waters of the Nolichucky River below and immediately knew that I would be soaking my feet in it as soon as I arrived.

The town has some businesses on the main road where the trail crosses that cater to adventurers. There are a few pubs, restaurants, and other neat little stores. Once you get across the street, there is a walking bridge with the AT insignia on it that crosses the Nolichucky. I saw Alpine there, and we talked about the last few days. I had seen her and Neil at Wayah Bald, where we got a few pictures of each other by the river.

I dropped my pack, sat down on a soft rock, and took my shoes and socks off. Alpine followed suit and we went to the water's edge and stuck our feet in the soothing waters. Then biting cold water caused synapses to fire like a reporter pounding on a keyboard after Watergate.

As my feet got used to the cold, I dipped more of my body in gradually. Alpine and I talked about tomorrow being our first "zero day"[7] since starting out. We had hiked 140 miles since meeting the initial few steps of Georgia. She continued to show encouragement to me, and I appreciated her positive influence on my adventure.

It was midday, and there was an area where other hikers gathered on a patio with tables and chairs not so far away. It was nice to sit in the warm sun on the patio overlooking the gorgeous river. While listening to each other's stories, knowing that each one of us was out on this journey for so many different reasons, whether it be heartache of some kind, a complete loss of faith in humanity, an illness, or loss of a loved one, we, each and every one of us, were in the here and now. We were not strangers; we were one, alive with nature within a substructure created by western civilization that, whether right or wrong, was ubiquitous. Like a giant snowball slicing down a precipitous cliff. No stopping it, just accepting certain percentages of it.

While we were hanging out, a hiking friend, named The Camel, said he was going to get a cabin or attempt to speak to the rental agency later in the evening to get a better deal. He was a good negotiator. By the end of the night, a dozen hikers were drinking cold beers (except me, of course). The comedy continued on the back deck, where Greenlite told a story while I played my ukulele. Another hiker, by the name of Moose, recorded the whole thing for posterity, but I believe she may have deleted it.

The next day was going to be a zero day. Yote and I roomed together. He is a very cool guy, and I was happy to be sharing his company.

We woke up the next morning and had an excellent breakfast. The lot of us had killed a few hours before we had to check out for the next guests to enjoy the cool cabin. I walked around town alone for a while and eventually went to the outfitters. After speaking with some nice people in town, they explained that the US kayaking team

---

[7] A "zero day" is when no miles are hiked on trial. It doesn't mean there aren't miles hiked back and forth from the stores, parties, restaurants, etc. It is supposed to be a break, but sometimes it doesn't feel like it when there are several chores to accomplish.

was going to be practicing on the river. I thanked the nice people and walked to the river to see about a dozen kayakers doing stunts in the white wash of the rapids.

Later, I walked back over to the patio where we were the day before. It became a hiker haven of sorts, and we became the welcoming committee for the other hikers who were arriving from the trail. A fellow hiker bought all of us trail magic pizza for lunch, and we sat there in our contentedness of sunshine and happiness. We hung out for several hours before hiking up the river with our packs to find a place to camp.

The outdoor center had three tents set up on pads for hikers to use with a pretty cool fire pit that surrounded it. We had a crew of about eight hikers, and all of us enjoyed laughter, a beautiful campfire, and good food.

I was organized and ready to go the next morning. When I arrived at the river, I took it in for a while before heading back out on the trail. The trail's ascent was somewhat grueling, but I pushed up the mountainside like I would have to do several hundred more times.

We came to some trail magic before hiking up Jacob's Ladder. I hiked a few miles to the next shelter with a hiking friend who was having a knee issue. I know the feeling. Having played football in high school, I know the trouble as we get older from stupid injuries from our youth.

The day before we got news two feet of snow had dumped on parts of the Smoky National Park. A few Appalachian Trail hikers needed rescuing off the mountains. Being less than fifty miles from that area was not reassuring for some of us, but we pressed on.

It was a restful night of sleep, but I was still slow to pack up and leave. I would often be the last person to leave the shelters when I went to bed "on time," or between eight and ten. The two days leading into Fontana Dam were relatively uneventful. The atmosphere was changing a bit in regards to the moving of the Earth and winter turning to spring. Spring smells better than what my olfactory nerves do to me in winter. When there is snow, the smell is fresh and clean. No snow, then to me, the end of winter smells of decaying death and rotting animals that have died.

I got to the road that leads into the village of Fontana, and a note on the information building said I could call for a ride. I just needed to get into town for my resupply food and maps. Then I could return right back to the trail and head my happy ass into the southern terminus of the Smoky National Forest.

I waited about thirty minutes and saw some other hiking friends continuing up the trail, deciding against a trip into town. First Gear and her cousin left up the trail as I was waiting, and we had some laughs. I played some music and sang for them as they moved farther into the forest.

My ride arrived, and I explained to the nice lady driver that I only needed to get to the post office to pick up my resupply. She was accepting of this information, but she took the ultra-long way, giving me a tour of some of the businesses in the village and explaining what they offered. I kindly said that I just needed to get to the post office. It was almost ten in the morning, so I thought I could get in and get out of this place that reminded me of the movie *House of Wax*. Sorry Fontana Dam, damn it . . . I just was sore and grumpy. No offense to anyone. I'm sure if I return I will stay at the hotel and go to all the stores.

At around this point is when she dropped the bomb on me. "The post office has new hours; they won't open until noon today."

I sat fuming for a bit when we pulled into the country store. Luckily, there were some hiking buds on the porch for me to vent to. I quickly grabbed my pack and got out, handed her the fare, and thanked her for the ride.

The post office opened and Yote and I got our packages. We shared some goodies and ate on the front porch of the country store. The rocking chairs were rather comfortable for weary hikers. I packed my food supply away, donned pack, and said good-bye to my pals. I got a ride back to the trail head with a few other hikers back to where we each got off the trail. I made sure that I went back to the last spot on the trail as a purist. I was pleased when I would make up even the Ys at shelters, instead of taking the shorter route. It was a fun and rewarding experience up until this point, and I was not going to change it up.

I got dropped off at the building with the phone to call the shuttle and some people were there just making the call when we pulled up. They were happy to see the ride into the village, as they just descended to the road from the mountain. I hiked up a short incline and saw water lapping the edge of a small hill to my right and heard the traffic from the road to my left. I hiked to the start of the Fontana Dam and the Little Tennessee River far below the monstrous concrete structure. It is still the largest dam on the east coast. In my mind I could recall the day's hike into the village and I could see the dam from about eight miles out. Regarding the structure for over two hours of hiking was king of annoying. When I first saw the dam, I thought, "Hey, there it is. We're almost there." The mirages on the Appalachian Trail are real.

The wind whipped in differing strengths as I crossed the concrete dam. It was closed to traffic when I passed, luckily, so it was quiet and very peaceful. As I looked up to the new budding of hundreds of trees and the experienced the smell of pine in my nostrils, I realized that this was going to be a painful evening if I was going to make the first shelter. Once I crossed the bridge, I took some time to look at my map, drink some water, and eat another small snack.

The Appalachian Trail follows one of the paved park roads until it cuts to the left up a steady incline. There was a box about twenty yards from the road along the earthen path that thru-hikers were required to put their twenty-dollar proof of permits into. I and my hiking friends were not happy about this, but a good percentage of us did pay the fee so we would not be in trouble if the park rangers stopped us and asked us for our permits. (They would later repeal this.)

The 2,189 foot hike up Shuckstack Mountain wore me out a great deal. I wanted to hike to the fire tower, but that was not going to happen. An agonizing 1.3 miles after the summit of Shuckstack, I came to a short one hundred-yard hike into a camping area and did my evening rituals. The next morning, a hiking pal arrived to get water as I was eating. I offered him some of my grub and he accepted. My resupply was heavy, and eating the extra weight would help me on my five thousand-foot elevation crushing of my mental and physical capabilities.

Once we were done eating, we started out up the mountain yet again. I was running out of water when I hit Molly's Ridge Shelter. I dropped my pack deliberately and grabbed my container and bee lined it to the water source. The water was coming down off the top of the mountain and looked so delicious. I did filter the water and headed over to the shelter to rest for a bit. Drenched in sweat, I asked myself, "Self, what the hell are you doing?"

I walked around the gorgeous area. The sunrays were shooting straight lines down in the grassy areas around the shelter. The trees were still in their initial stages of budding out for spring, and the smells of decay were absconding. As I walked back to the shelter, a light sprinkle began to hit the ground. My buddy from England, Limey as I nicknamed him earlier on, was water getting when the sprinkles turned cold and hard. We got cover and were safe inside the shelter when the massive hailstorm erupted before our very eyes. The storm only lasted for five to ten minutes before the sun came out again. It was Mother Nature giving us a show, and it was nothing short of magnificent. I had only hiked five miles, but I needed to reserve my energy for the rest of the grueling Smoky Mountains.

The next morning, my mental capacities were somewhat making a comeback, and I donned pack and headed back out on the trail. As the elevations rose and fell over the next three miles to Russell Field Shelter, the winds were kicking up in an ebb and flow. Sometimes more flow, like a hair dryer flow. The weather was cold and damp. I was lucky it was not sleet or hail. I met a nice hiker from Boston whom I began hiking with. I called him Boston, but he had another trail name that unfortunately I don't recall. He hiked ahead of me before Spence Field Shelter. Because the shelter was over a quarter of a mile off of the Appalachian Trail, I moved on after a bite to eat and a sip of water.

The rains began when I climbed over Old Rocky Top. I actually had that song ready to play on the Hinkele when I arrived, but the rains would not allow it. "Good Ol' Rocky Top . . . Rocky Top Tennesseeeee!" I moved on, literally hiking in the clouds. The summit at 5,527 feet of Thunderhead Mountain was somewhat eventful as the clouds parted in places, leaving some openings to the ridged valley below. It was super cool to witness the perpetual changes in front of my face piece.

Country music stars sing a lot about this area of The Great Smoky Mountain Range. I knew Johnny Cash had hiked where I was hiking. Dolly Parton grew up not far away, and in my mind I knew she probably also made several appearances on some of the more famous trails. At least I hoped so anyway. All celebrities should hike; it's the last significant vestige for all human folk. It was pretty humbling to be in the presence of so many American giants, at any rate.

I arrived at Derrick Knob Shelter in the evening, where the first thing I saw was bear hangers about thirty yards from the shelter. Some hikers were already in the process of hanging their foodstuff. The line connected to a tree where hikers could lower their food down to the ground. I only hung my food if someone asked me to. I understood some people were very paranoid about a bear attack. Otherwise, my bear bag was always my pillow. Midnight cravings happened from time to time.

After I had eaten a good supper, I played some ukulele with Jebidiah Jambo. I was still somewhat learning to play along my journey, but I wasn't horrible. Whenever anyone wanted to play, I would say with a jovial burst, "This is a community, uke!" Some of the hikers who played her were good, and some people wanted a lesson. I gave those folks a short tutorial and watched them light up when they would play something that sounded pretty good. We all would smile and laugh, knowing that instruments and music, in general, are equivalent to food when it came to a common ground for the human condition. Sure politics and religion would come up in the discussion, but food and ukulele never caused people to walk away from a conversation.

The Derrick Knob Shelter was in good condition. It was two levels for sleeping around twelve people. Walking into the shelter, I saw the dirt floor area was narrow. Several backpack hangers were placed evenly around the walls. There was a lovely fireplace and a fire warming folks and drying out their socks and wet boots.

The fire was going for most of the night. Before going to bed, I was reading the *Adventures of Tom Sawyer* and was asked if I would mind reading aloud. I did not mind. I read that very book to the kids I worked with several times over in the course of the nine years at the day school. I read three chapters, put the book away, and went to sleep.

The fire was smoldering during the night, and I saw a hiker fanning the smoke, but no flame was coming from it. I felt dizzy and needed air. I was sleeping very close to the fireplace. I jumped out of my bag and began coughing while walking out of the shelter. I sat in the crisp air, looking up to an incredible starry night. Once the coughing subsided, I went back into the still smoky theater of the shelter. I moved my head farther away from the hiker still fanning the smoke. I stated to him that he was only making it worse, but he ignored me. I lay my head down and fell back to sleep.

The next morning I was not feeling well, more than likely from smoke inhalation. I decided to stay at the Derrick Knob shelter one more night before heading out in the morning. Getting sick in the wilderness is no fun. I drank plenty of water, and someone offered me some powdered vitamin C. Within a few hours, I was feeling much better. The day saw many hikers either continue their adventure or set up their camping areas and stay for the night.

Clouds came in and another storm hit hard in the open field. Around the shelter thunder could be heard in the distance. A few section hikers came into a full shelter with their muddy boots and began making demands of the hikers in the shelter, saying, "We have permits!" There were three of them, and they were more than rude to folks who hiked over one hundred miles to be in the safety of the shelter.

Technically, the last three thru-hikers were to leave the shelter and allow the entitled section hikers their right sleeping areas in regards to The Smoky Mountains National Park guidelines. The last three people who settled in were still wet to the bone from the storm. One of the section hikers stood at the base of my sleeping bag with his muddy boots getting close to my things. I sat up, looked at this guy, and then I took my hand and sprayed the mud back onto him. I stood up, and the air in the shelter changed. I told him that I would give up my space for them. I was feeling somewhat better, and I did not want to be angry. This guy had the nerve to come into the area thinking he could kick out anyone because they had "permits." I wanted to say, "Hey douche nugget, we have permits, too!" But he was drawled up and ready for a confrontation. When some other hikers heard the commotion from outside, they received the details. They were not pleased with the circumstances and laughed at my diatribe of the situation.

I went back into the shelter and stated to the three section hikers that the next time they come into a situation like that, they should not show a dominant power over people who were exhausted; instead, they should come in and say, "Hello," and explain that they had three spaces reserved and were not sure what should happen and ask if the folks in the shelter could get it sorted out, then say they would appreciate that. Jagoffs were running around town.

Boston, I, and Machete were the ones who went out in the weather and set up our tents. My tent being the water holder, I found a somewhat bed of pine needles under a shelter of pine branches. The night was windy, but the rain subsided, thankfully for me.

I slept well, and the next morning I hiked by myself for a while over some fantastic forest area. The clouds came and went several times over the course of my hike. It was a short hiking day to Double Spring Gap Shelter because I still was not feeling up to snuff, as some hikers say, but even still, that hike was a strenuous climb.

The Double Spring Gap Shelter was three sided, and the winds were whipping in the front of the shelter. There was a tarp set up, but it was flapping and shredded in several places. I had a tarp, and we set to closing ourselves into the shelter. It worked well, and my trail friends, Ripper, Mud Flap, Mud Slide, and Future, gathered some wood for a fire. I was just hoping that the smoke did not hinder me for the next day's hike to the highest point on the Appalachian Trail.

We sat around, chatting and enjoying the ruggedness of our surroundings. The privy, or where we all go to do "poopy doopy time," was open for a view of the ridgeline and mountains in the distance. Several of us would take pictures of this privy and come to find it was a very attractive place to snap a few funny shots of people doing their business.

Chapter FIVE

I was feeling different, my body was changing, even in the short period of hiking, and I was getting stronger. With pack donned after finishing up necessities, I hiked with Mud Slide to the top of Clingmans Dome.

Clingmans Dome stood at over 6,600 feet. We were greeted by some very nice section hikers who were giving away their leftover food that they didn't need. It was some really good stuff. Mud Slide needed more food than I did, so I took one of the meals and he took two. We made our way up the paved walkway to stellar views. These were earned views, more so than when folks drive up and see the sights. It wouldn't be until New Hampshire and the White Mountains that I was taught by my trail friend, Beowulf, that these folks are known as "goofers."

Mud Slide walked the mile down the paved road to the gift shop, hoping to get some more food for the next leg of the Smoky Mountains. He would be disappointed. He bought a bag of corn meal and a few candy bars. He gave me a candy bar and I asked him how he was going to prepare the corn meal. I told him he needed some pasta sauce and mozzarella cheese. He did not have those things, so bland cooked corn meal it would have to be.

I spent a few more minutes staring out into the great expanse where I just had come from. I could see Standing Indian Mountain and thought about Patchouli and hoped she was well. There were several other mountains in the distance, and I could feel the power in my legs to get moving to the next shelter before the sunset for the night.

It was a poor mileage day for me to the Mount Collins Shelter because of the awesome views of the dome. Luckily for me, I was around great people and nature. No control tube or commercials to tell me what to buy or do. Thrift stores are people too. Thanks, Citizens United!

I read aloud the *Adventures of Tom Sawyer* for the next several shelters and assisted my fellow hikers to sleep. Shelter TV at its finest. The ukulele came out every once in a while. Because I did not have an ear for tuning, I would often have to get out a tuner or ask some musically inclined folks who knew how to for assistance.

Davenport Gap is the only road crossing of the entire Appalachian Trail throughout the wilderness of the Great Smoky Mountains. I got out the ukulele, and trail magic came from some nice folks traveling through. Some homemade oatmeal cookies, a few Gatorades, and beef jerkies—my hiking families were all around me to imbibe in the caloric intake for the next leg.

Although some hikers did decide to mosey on into town, I had heard to bypass that city and keep on going unless I wanted to see a human circus fitted with costly amusement and ads everywhere the eye could see. Concrete and guns . . . electricity and pollution . . . not my bag.

The views leaving Davenport Gap were excellent. The Ice Water Shelter was set on a bluff with a rock-star status view fit for a king or queen. Girls hiking the AT were some of the strongest humans I have ever witnessed. I just wanted to put the myth to rest that some women cannot hike the miles that men can. I mean, have you not heard of Jennifer Pharr Davis? If not, get on it; she is an inspiration to everyone everywhere. Great person and great author. I digress, again. But yeah, Women! Rock! I would like to share my life with one someday. Forever, she is out there; I just have to find her. Or she has to find me. I didn't see her at Charlie's Bunion when I walked there from the Ice Water Shelter, but it does not mean she was not close.

Charlie's Bunion is a rock formation that looked like a bunion on some old guy's foot, as it was named. The rock formation that makes up this weirdly named area overlooks folds and folds of mountain ranges and over the crest of the mountains that fall and climb into an astonishing reality of the smallness of we people. The reminder that no human has absolute control over the big blue ball. So sweet that knowledge is power.

Ice Water Shelter would hold a little something extra in the reading of Tom Sawyer because a hiker pal, who was a gifted music artist, played my ukulele while I read. It was quite the experience for all of us. I could have read more, but because reading aloud a great deal and the inhalation smoke thing was still bothering me, I was becoming a bit horse. Many people were sleepy, too, and needed their rest for the next day's gruel.

I was an early riser the next morning. I trudged along an impressive thirteen miles for the elevation, and several mountains ascended and descended like a boss. The Tri-Knob Shelter was fun, and I was only a few chapters short of finishing Tom Sawyer, but someone requested that I start from the beginning again. "TOM! Hey, YOU, TOM?"

The next day's hike was almost fifteen miles and complete with the Smoky Mountains. Seventy-one miles of the Smoky's were done, accomplished, conquered. To say it felt good would be an incredible understatement. I was seen running down the mountain into the Davenport Shelter. My strides were long, and my voice was loud and bois- terous to the annoyance of my fellow hikers. I apologized for my wildness, but some- times people have to let that energy out, or it builds up and instead out comes anger. I get it. Go somewhere wild and yell out with all of your might. Do it! It feels mighty good.

I made it an early night to bed at the Davenport Shelter. This three-sided building is one of the few fenced-in shelters because I suppose bear were worse there. I was wet, tired, and somewhat cranky. A quick dinner, and to bed I went without much fanfare.

Then next morning, I hiked the road walks across the Pigeon River and then a few miles to The Standing Bear Hostel. When I walked up the dirt road, there was a neat little layout of camping areas and small cabins with a hiker kitchen, hiker resupply area, and some pretty nice backcountry folk. They made me feel like family. A bit strange for the more urban fellowship, but their kindness was prevalent as soon as I walked in. There was an offer of community grub, and I happily accepted. I sat and chatted with some of my hiker trash family. "Hiker trash" is a term of endearment for hikers of the trail.

I was going to stay, but when I looked at the map, there was a big climb ahead, and I wanted to get that checked off my Appalachian Trails miles before the sun set. The hike out of the hostel was a bit tiresome as I climbed back up to the thinning air. I was still feeling somewhat blah when I arrived at the first fresh water spring, so I made a primitive camp of it.

A few hiker friends I hadn't seen in a while, but who recognized my tent, yelled out to me, "Uke?" I poked my head out of the little pup tent and said hello to Low Rider. Low Rider is from Estonia. His family owns a farm there, and he was out exploring America the right way. Like one should cook a pork shoulder or other succulent meats . . . slowly. He stopped and visited while another hiker, named Cat, who also hiked with a ukulele, stopped by and serenaded us an original song she wrote. The two of them hiked on, and I went to lullaby land.

I woke up the next morning and walked hard to Brown Gap because there was mention of some trail magic that would not disappoint. Before Brown Gap is the side trail to the Groundhog Creeks Shelter. The climb was hard at this point and my hiking pal, Jedidiah Jambo, came out and searched for me with only his guitar, singing a song about trail magic. It was such an uplifting gesture for him to come and see not only how I was doing, but also to show that significant amount of support for me. I felt much loved at that moment and hiked hard into the Rat Pack trail magic at Brown Gap. I told Jedidiah that I appreciated his singing in the last quarter mile to the trail magic, which was something I will never forget.

The dual wheel truck was in a Y of three dirt roads. There were two large tents behind a large covered trailer. One of the tents had several chairs and weary hikers' asses in them. I received a warm greeting and a deviled egg after I had set my pack down. Rat and his crew brought enough food for an entire army for the weekend. His guitar and funny songs around the campfire at night and laughter were of great importance for not only me, but for our whole hiking community that lived in the magic bubble they created for us in 2013.

The magical meals consisted of: hams, sausages, pork chops, steaks, ground beef, so many assorted vegetables, fruits, and legumes, scrambled eggs with cheese and sautéed veggies, and kielbasa.

They brought enough food and drinks for all the hiker trash that were already there and some who were still arriving.

Rat made an announcement on the first day: "Ladies and Gentlemen, I am sorry to ruin your hiking experience. We will serve a great bounty this entire weekend. You are more than welcome to stay all three days, but we understand if you have to go. But you will miss some great food, great stories, and a trail experience that will go down as the best on trail." We had our fill of life, food, and so much positive energy.

I met many more hikers at the Brown Gap trail magic than the several miles previous. Many hikers were there whom I did know from passing, and when I say passing, I mean them passing me. The next three days of hiking was a wash, but not in a bad way. There was a consistent drizzle and light rain that never really let up. A few hikers made an impressive bonfire. The fire was so hot that the rain was dissipating before it had a chance to hit the ground. It was a wet, yet incredible, weekend experience on the backcountry roads of Tennessee.

.

On my last night, my tent became drenched, as well as my down sleeping bag. I went over to Rat and asked if I could bunk with him in his van. He was not too gung ho on the idea, but he was a compassionate man. He even kept the van running with the heat on so my sleeping bag dried out. The smells from my sleeping bag that imparted into his van were less than pleasant, though. He was cool about it because he also is a great adventurer and knows these types of situations are prevalent in the rigors of trail life.

It was hard leaving before lunch on the last day of the magic, but a new hiker friend from Boston and I hiked on late morning and began a partly cloudy day's walk over a famous bald mountain, known as Max Patch. People married on this large grassy mountain for its incredible views and overall grandeur.

We hiked hard up and over the Max Patch Summit, Walnut Mountain, and Bluff Mountain. We took short breaks and pushed our bodies to the limit. We were only a few miles from Hot Springs, North Carolina, when I explained to Boston that I didn't think I could go on. The insides of my thighs chaffed liked two Virginia hams cooked close together. It was only another three miles to the road, and he convinced me that I could make it. It was getting dark, and I was moving slowly, but I agreed that I could make it. Also, I knew that I was going to be taking a day off the next day, so that propelled me down the steep Deer Park Mountain.

The sun set fast before we put on our headlamps to descend the rocky terrain of the path. We heard some loud voices and behind us came hopping Survivor and Nuke, both jovial fellows who were headed into town, as well. Nuke also carried a ukulele and was going with the trail name Uke, but instead was named New-Uke, shortened to Nuke. He was an excellent musician and fun to hang around. Survivor was just that; he was smart and great company. He and Nuke traveled a lot together in towns and along the trail.

I wanted to kiss the concrete when we arrived at the parking area at the base of the mountain. I think maybe I had. We just hiked twenty-three miles—the most miles I have ever lifted in the course of fewer than twelve hours, let alone an entire day, ever, in my life.

The hostel was directly in front of us with its welcoming lights. When I reached the front porch, my body had given its last, and I dropped without taking my pack off on the hostel steps. Boston said he would search out the manager and find us some beds or a room or a shower or a back rub or a hot tub or just a hot bath with Epsom salts included. I told him I'd wait. I could feel my heartbeat in my thighs, and I was falling asleep right there where I lay.

As I was nodding off, I heard Boston talking to someone a few yards away.

"No, nothing available for tonight. Why didn't you call ahead? I could have let you know," the manager stated to Boston.

"Is there anything at all in town?" Boston asked.

"No, really there is nothing. You guys can set up your tents over by the—"

"Hello!" I said, desperation in my voice.

The manager looked down at my corpse-looking body sitting on his front steps. "Hi," he said, reluctant to get into a conversation with me.

"I'm Uke." I exhaled the words through exhaustion.

"Wait. You're Uke?" he asked.

"Yes, sir. And I would—"

"Hold on. I'll be right back."

Boston and I looked at one another, but I was too tired to talk. The manager's name was Chuck Norris. No, not *the* Chuck Norris, but he was a pretty intimidating guy, so I am sure he had some of the same characteristics as *the* Chuck Norris. Maybe minus flying heel kicks and things.

It seemed like forever that he was gone, but he came back and stated that some hiker pals of mine vouched for my existence on the Appalachian Trail, and there was room on the chapel floor for me.

"What about him?" I pointed to Boston.

"Yeah, him too," Chuck Norris replied.

"Thank you, thank you, thank you, thank you!" I exclaimed as I peeled myself from my concrete tomb.

Boston and I met our hiker friends with smiles and congratulations. I chided them on taking a ride from Max Patch, but they were going to run pretty much a marathon the next day in a slack pack. Slack pack means you only carry water and snacks along the trail and destroy trail miles without carrying twenty or more pounds. It's pretty intense because even though the miles seem to be easier, when the time comes when it is necessary to carry all the weight for an extended period, it becomes a lot more difficult. Well, for some people.

It was a zero day the next day, but getting out of my wet clothes and lugging my sore ass to the shower after Boston was through was difficult, but important. After my piping hot shower, I slid into the sleeping bag for the night. I was handed a Snickers before I went to bed by an awesome hiker girl who was a very kind, caring soul. I thanked her, swallowed the candy bar in seconds, and was soon sawing the proverbial log. Thank you guys for telling Chuck Norris I was an okay person. Little did he know. Wink.

The next morning was a glorious sunny day with huge, shiny, white puffy clouds rising into the atmosphere like several bulbous steps. I wandered into town and stopped at a local eatery along the way. A Reuben sandwich was calling my name, and I was happy with my decision.

Sitting at a bar in town, I noticed they had tables and chairs right on the river, so I moved. Being closer to the soothing sounds of rushing water drifted some of my anxieties out of my mind. I spent the next several hours watching hikers come and go. Some would stop and drink beer in front of me. That frothy goodness of a thing, staring me down like three hundred pounds of leather-wearin' biker men. Seeing the hoppy cold brew, I realized that there was no way I was not making it to Maine. Double negative much? Yes, yes I will. I thought to myself, "I cannot believe I gave up beer!" It gets worse before it gets better, as I was still very far away from Mount K and the glorious wilderness of Maine.

Back at the hostel on a beautiful sunny afternoon, I was able to visit with Leslie, Ali, and Rich. They told us of a house they rented with a Jacuzzi. They were hiking out but said if we wanted to see if the room was available, it was worth it.

Boston and I already got a room with beds inside and a shower close by for our zero days. I looked over my pack and made some adjustments, knowing that I would have another heavy bag by leaving with another full load. It was a noisy night in the hostel, but certain aspects of trail life are.

The next morning was excellent; I was somewhat slow in moving around because I was still quite sore from the hike into Hot Springs. I met some hiker pals for breakfast and saw a few other hikers heading into town. Town days are so fun when you're a long-distance hiker freak. Our community is so friendly; when we see each other, it's as if we see long lost friends by our big hand waves above our heads and yelps and yowls of knowing that what we are doing is one of the most exhilarating experiences . . . ever.

I tried to convince Boston to hike out with me, but he felt he needed another zero day in town. I continued with a light breeze across the city of Hot Springs, North Carolina. It is the only North Carolina town that the Appalachian Trail goes through. In fact, the sidewalks have fresh AT markers on the town path. A neat city, very cool people—I suggest everyone visit Hot Springs, North Carolina. The walk back to where Boston and I got off the trail was a bit of a backtrack for me. But I was already in my head on the purist part of it. Again, I am sorry if you were offended by me. It was not an easy way, especially in the eyes of the beer holders. Through town, on aptly named Bridge Street, across the rushing waters of Spring Creek and toward the stampeding waters of the French Broad River, the Appalachian Trail sneaks down along the river before shooting up into the sky and landing at an amazing overlook of Hot Springs, called Lovers Leap Rock. I snapped a few cool shots of the rushing river before moving along.

I hiked around a very nice family from Florida; I would see them off and on through the back and forth of North Carolina and Tennessee along the border of each state. The trail pulled into Virginia, the longest border-to-border hiking along the Appalachian Trail.

The trail meanders up 3,500 feet to a mountain, called Rich Mountain (which is exactly what anyone feels after climbing that beast from Lovers Leap). A thru-hiking German, cool guy, named Peewee German, and I camped in the Rich Mountain Fire Tower. We were surprised the next morning with swift fog clouds whipping through the open-aired fire tower. The wind was a bit chilly, but we coped well. The Bard and her ma were hiking together and were from Wisconsin. They were friendly people, and I enjoyed the Bard's love of Bob Dylan. I am also a big fan of him.

After a descent of more than a thousand feet, the path leads to several gaps before another grueling climb of 4,750 feet. The ridgeline the next ten miles is relaxing enough. The trail phone (a.k.a. hikers talking to hikers), said there was going to be a cold front coming into Erwin, Tennessee. It was supposed to be quite daunting.

I had done the climb over Big Bald at 5,500 feet and down through Big Stamp before I reached Bald Mountain Shelter for a quick bite. While I was sitting there, a thru-hiker by the name of Mailman from Virginia stopped to eat. The wind was starting to destroy the brown tarp attached to the front of the shelter. The tarp did little to keep out the cold.

"Are you going to stay here?" Mailman asked.

"Uh, no, and you shouldn't either."

"I was going to."

"It is going to be freezing here tonight. You should head down the mountain with me now. The weather will get warmer the lower in elevation we get."

"Okay."

Mailman and I escaped the shelter and began the drop through Little Bald, across two footbridges, until we hit Spivey Gap. We could have continued, but Erwin was calling our names. A town stop and the mention of pizza is Pavlovian for a thru-hiker. We quickly got a ride from a day-hiking couple into Erwin.

Erwin was a two-day, storm-dodging hotel stay with my new hiking pal, Mailman. Mailman and I stunk up the hotel room with our fresh, musky hiker smell. We had a good time and a lot of great laughs while being holed up, watching the skies above the mountain turn mean with gray color and angry sounds. I would see First Gear and her cousin at the hotel and hang out with them for a few hours before heading back to my room to see what Mailman was doing.

I picked up several packages of goodies from family and friends. I received a new pair of trekking poles from my mom. The poles I was using to this point were trashed from 331 miles of abuse. I picked up foodstuff from Aunt Gin and Uncle Tim, Cousin Jennifer, Robby, Lucas, and Robyn, and some wonderful letters of encouragement.

Mailman got sick with what many hikers became ill with: dun dun dun . . . the noro-virus! This virus was a very contagious illness. He and I were sharing close quarters together. I decided to let him rest while I hiked from Spivey Gap to an incredible view of the Nolichucky River. Miss Janet, one of the most remarkable trail angels on the AT, drove me and a fellow hiker, named Little Bear, to the trailhead at Spivey Gap.

The eleven miles went pretty quickly over the crisp mountain folds before descending with a view and rumbling sound of the Nolichucky River below. The trail was kind and forgiving. The stream crossings held fresh, rich waters. The sun showed between inter-mittent puffs of clouds that passed across the Carolina blue sky.

There was a superfluity of hikers at the Uncle Johnny's Hostel, where Little Bear and I waited for Miss Janet. I arrived back to our hotel room in time to hear Mailman blowing chunks in the hotel bathroom. I asked him if he was okay and he said he was getting better. Yeah, sounded like it. I was worried about him, but I knew he would be back into the saddle as soon as he was ready. He decided on one more day in the hotel, and I decided to hike on.

On my way, I was quickly passed by the Warrior Hikers. Some of them knew me from trail stories when they saw my ukulele. They introduced themselves, and I met Jabba, Flow, Momma Goose, and a myriad of other inspiring veterans. Meeting them and hiking with them were two different things because their pace was that of a double time cadence of mine, although somewhat faster from my AT beginnings, yet nowhere near their ability.

Mailman introduced me to Mama Chip, whose daughter, Chipmunk, was attempting a solo thru-hike as the youngest to achieve the accolade at fourteen when she began. Her strength was reassuring and hopefully inspiring to girls growing up with any stigma they may be dealing with. Whenever I would see Chipmunk on a certain day's hike and then run into her mom, I would always tell her that she was not far away and kicking ass. Mama Chip was always kind and cheerful. Many times she offered soda, a ride, a shoulder, a hug, and overall she was pretty much rock 'n' roll, and anyone who said otherwise was just a tool bag. I would quickly meet Chipmunk for the first time on the hike out of Erwin. I told her I met her ma, and she said yeah that she had heard that Mailman jackrabbited himself ahead to make it to Trail Days. Although I missed hiking with him, he was much faster than me, and I was not trying to hold anyone up from getting their hike complete.

Unaka Mountain and its dense spruce forest smelled clean and crisp. The weather was nice with gusts of wind at times. I saw the hiker crew dubbed the Sun Gods. They included K-Biz, Wicked-Miner, Schnitzel, Dutch, Jolly Green Giant, Mamacita, Angry Bird, and Teen Wolf. They enjoyed being as safe as possible on trail. We enjoyed chiding each other. That group was some awesome hiker folk. I would hike near them for the remainder of the trail.

Chapter SIX

The hiking in and out of North Carolina and Tennessee would be some difficult miles, but very picturesque and beautiful miles. I made a slow pace of the trail through the Roan Mountain range. I camped with Twenty-Two, Push-Up, and my trail parents at Stan Murray Shelter. K-Biz stopped by and talked to us for a bit. Twenty-two and Push-up were great hikers from Georgia. During our conversation with K- Biz, a small, I think it was a Pomeranian, dog that a weekend family had in their camp lifted its leg on K-Biz's pack and urinated. I made a joke.

"Instead of K-Biz, you'll from here forth be called, K9 Pissy."

"No, don't do that." Then K-Biz kicked that dog halfway down the mountain. (Just kidding, but I knew it was going through his mind because he told me so years later.)

Although it was funny, K-Biz did not find it that funny. So, I did not call him K9 Pissy anymore. The camp at Stan Murray had a few laughs, though. K-Biz hiked on with dog urine on his pack while we all prepared for bed. Twenty-Two was telling me how Push-up carried two bottles, one for water and one to piss in when he needed to go. She said it matter-of-factly, but stated,

"Sometimes he forgets which one he used for water and ends up drinking out of his piss bottle."

"You don't kiss him do you?" I asked.

The impressive barn, named the Over Mountain Shelter, transformed into a shelter, where I met Little Spoon and Chuckles. Chuckles and Little Spoon are a couple from New Hampshire and are some pretty amazing folks who, again, I had a bunch of fun with that included mostly laughter and snarky snarks sarcasm stuff conversations.

The Over Mountain Shelter is only a few miles away from the Stan Murray Shelter, but I felt I needed to stay at the enormous hiker shelter. The barn had a privy you could poop in, with a mountain view! Yes, all privies you can poop in, but some you have to hover over if they are crowning. Not a pleasant sight. Luckily when I did my poopy doopy time in the privy at the barn shelter, it was clean and scenic to boot.

All in the fun on the trail, but then again, I was very annoying sometimes, no doubt. I get that. I don't apologize because I am just one human with a lizard brain that makes mistakes, and my mistakes don't cause physical harm or, at least, I hope not. Moving on!

The hike after the barn was unbelievably beautiful. The exposed areas of the Roan Mountains are, well, let me just say that I spread my arms apart with the high winds hitting my face, singing, "The hills are alive with the sound of music . . ."

Gorgeous! We had a great hike into the small community of Roan Mountain, North Carolina. A little hitch there and off to the right was a restaurant called Bob's Dairyland.

Upon entering Bob's Dairyland, Chuckles ordered first.

"I'll have the Holy Cow Burger, please . . . and is there any chance you could add a fried egg on top?" she asked.

The lady taking the order tried to discourage this type of behavior but agreed that a fried egg could come on the burger for an extra charge.

"That's what I want," she said confidently.

"Make that two," I said. Or Little Spoon said. Perhaps we said it together.

I could research that with them, but it'll be available in the comments below the reviews for this trash. By the way, I will never read the comments. I was told never to read the comments. So I won't. You can't hurt my feelings, the world!

The Holy Cow Burger add fried egg was like magical fairy food made just for our hungry hiker bellies. The burger came with a steak knife! Piled high on a skewer were three beef patties, three slices of their very own sugar cured ham, a handful of hickory smoked bacon, two kinds of cheese, lettuce, tomato, mayo, and onion. You'd think that would be it, enough to feed a small family of four, but no . . . a scoop of their house chili on the bottom burger bun, two beer battered onion rings, and a partridge in a pear tree! Okay, minus the latter. But seriously, so good, so good we had to add a milkshake to all of our orders. It was magnificent . . . magnificent on a plate. The hike up the mountain after that meal was like dragging a brick in my belly. It was just about that time.

"Are we there yet? I have to go to the bathroom!"

"No, and stop asking if we're there yet. We'll get there when we get there."

"But?"

"No buts about it. Don't make me turn this car around."

"Ahhhhh!"

Levity and comedy led to the pain not feeling as, well, painful.

Fun with rhymes, fun with songs, fun with making shit up as we go along. Just to get the thought of aching body parts out of our mind. Any distraction to numb the pain was a good one. It worked.

There were a couple of neat scenic views and the sound of rushing water from water-falls along the trail that were pretty cool. Chuckles, Little Spoon, and I thought we were closer to our shelter destination than we were for a while, until we gave up thinking how close we were and made a hard climb and descent into the Mountaineering Shelter.

Toward the end of snaking through the two states, we came to the site of a lone grave and tombstone. The gravesite belonged to Nick Grindstaff, or Uncle Nick as the locals called him. Coincidentally, my friend, Andy, and his sons share lineage with Uncle Nick. Uncle Nick became a hermit in the mountains for forty years. The words on his tombstone read, "He lived alone, suffered alone, and died alone." Some hikers have said they have heard eerie happenings while camped out near Uncle Nick's grave.

My trail friends, Hightide and Blockade Runner, were there with me before I hiked into the road that would take me into Damascus, Virginia, for Trail Days. Trail Days is held annually for hikers from all walks of life. There are great, caring people in the town of Damascus, Virginia. Hightide and Blockade Runner were dubbed my trail parents in the Smoky Mountains. Every time I knew they were going to be in the same camp as me, I would make sure there was a fire ready for them when they arrived. I would enjoy many laughs and good times with them on the trail ahead.

Trail Days is a three-day hiking festival I was not going to miss for the world. I still had twenty-one miles to hike into the town of Damascus, but when I got to the road, I figured I could leave early on Sunday morning to walk back. The hitch into town was rather painless. There were already a few people in the parking area at the roadside.

A nice gentleman picked me up, and I asked him to drop me in the middle of town. I saw Low Rider, Limey, Boston, and several other hiking friends. I was specifically looking for Honey Badger, Kowabunga, and Vita-C when I heard someone call out my name. I was unfamiliar with the hiker, but she saw my ukulele and told me that Honey Badger was looking for me.

"The group is over at The Lazy Fox Inn."

"Okay. Thank you. See you later."

She gave me directions, and I began walking across town to the fabulous setting of this truly glorious establishment. The Laurel Creek sang its river song behind the old Victorian inn along East Imboden Street. The front of the house had a wraparound porch to the right of the inn and a gazebo to the back left. There was a large yard area both in the back and left of the inn. A sidewalk to the left of the house led you to the gazebo and the backyard. Three huge trees held two very relaxing hammocks held in place with large steel bolts, literally right next to Laurel Creek.

I heard Honey Badger calling my name as I walked toward the house. She came running and gave me a huge hug, which I so needed and so appreciated. The love of trail friends makes the whole experience that much more worthwhile. She took me back to the house as she was telling me how our fate led to the doorstep of one of the premier spots in town. She and Kowabunga arrived a day before the crowds came in and asked politely if they and some trail friends could tent camp in the yard adjacent to the inn. The innkeeper was happy to accommodate such kind and thoughtful people into her yard.

Honey Badger told me to pick out a spot and get comfortable while she went to town. Vita-C and Kowabunga were off trying to win some free gear in the Trail Days traditional hiker raffles that were held on the hour or sometimes several times per hour depending on the vendor's location.

I settled in by getting out of my stinky hiker clothes and into my camp shorts. The jump into the Laurel Creek that had been calling my name since the first time I laid my eyes on her was more than refreshing. She was a beauty, and she talked to me in the gentle kind of way that I like. Oh nature just does it to me.

Some hiker friends were over by the pavilion, and I walked over to meet some new faces and some that I knew of from some mile back I could not recall. Instruments were laid out on the picnic table, so I laid my ukulele down, as well, to fill the space. The positive energy from ukulele is a pretty powerful thing to feel.

For the next few hours, I walked around town, caught up to Boston, and he and I went for tacos at a local eatery. The tacos and company were good before I headed back to the inn for the evening.

Vita-C and Kowabunga were there and greeted each other with big hugs and "nice to see yous." The sun was heading down over the westerly mountains, and the instruments were coming to life, as well as the vocalists who enjoyed a good romp in the proverbial choir. Over a dozen people were in the gazebo while jams were being jammed. The music, laughter, singsong time was encompassed into the night and early morning hours of the next day. It was a beautiful night to be a part of, and if the next afternoon had not come, it would have been a weekend of great joy.

But the next afternoon did come. Several people in the morning asked me if I was going to the parade or if I was going to some of the raffles some of the vendors were having. I did go into town to some of the local suppliers, but I was not feeling well. A head cold and pounding headache would put me in for the next several hours. I took a Benadryl and two ibuprofen before falling fast asleep.

I woke up to stillness and quiet, except for the soft murmur of Laurel Creek. I poked my head out of my tent and saw a few fishermen in the water casting their bait to catch the storied fish. As I stood, I stretched and yawned; my head still hurt, but I needed food.

I put on my camp shoes and made my way to main street Damascus for some good grub from a restaurant that sold only the right, poison-less, foodstuff. Ahhh chicken noodle soup was on the menu and, yes, I wanted that with some fresh French loaf. Oh my goodness, smack yo granny.

The parade was just setting up, only a few blocks away from where I sat slurping my sustenance. Soup slopping on my beard and dribbling down my whiskers. I pretty much was free of judgmental eyes amongst "my people." My head still throbbed even after I took another ibuprofen. Each year a parade of past thru-hikers from different years walks with banners marking their particular year and so many other things that sets the hikers apart from previous years. Our class was toward the back of the parade with the hikers from the earlier class in front.

I was just finishing up eating when I heard the sirens wailing. I looked up and outside, and I saw waves of people heading in the direction of the parade. I was not sure what was going on, but I knew it was not good. I stood up and had to gain my balance, as now I felt somewhat dizzy. My body was making dramatic changes, and it had to catch up to what I was putting it through. The door to the café rung as I exited, and the first person I saw was a girl with crocodile tears and her mascara running down her cheeks. That was when I heard the helicopters in the air. One life flight was one thing—two, well that scared me, and I began shaking.

Immediately, I turned back into the café, making the bell ring again. I knew it was bad, and in my heart, I knew that it could be someone I had come to know through the last month and a half of hiking. No way was my mental capacity prepared for bad news regarding one of my hiking friends. Some people came in and gave us what the vine had given them, and many times accuracy with these sorts of things is a little hit and miss. Sometimes just hit and miss.

The blades cut the air like drummers by a fire. The talk continued inside the café to an annoying cadence for me. I left, this time heading back to the inn, where I was sure our group would meet and check that every one of us was uninjured and safe. I was allowing only positive vibes within my brain as I walked my damaged body the three blocks to the river and the inn.

When I arrived, there was a somber mood amongst everyone there. Vita-C was the first one I spoke to, and his reaction was mainly shocking. Approximately fifty hikers hit by an elderly man driving a Cadillac. Three people were life flighted, and thank the giant gummy bear that there were no fatalities.

"I'm outta here!" Vita-C stated.

Vita-C, Honey Badger, and Kowabunga were about forty miles ahead of me on the trail. He suggested that I go along with him and skip the forty miles. I was already in a routine that I could not abandon. I told him that I couldn't, best was to catch up with the group as soon as I could.

I could not argue with him for leaving, the whole of the hiker community in Damascus was in a bad way. The positivity of the entire weekend was being filled like a great big joy balloon only to be needled by an unfortunate accident. Like a child who has his or her first balloon, when it pops, it is not just sadness, but actual shock at the sound and sight that it contains. Oh, psychology . . . what you do to us.

It would not be long before several hiking friends decided the same thing. I stayed pretty much to myself for the rest of the day near the bosom of Laurel Creek, snuggled in the tranquility of one of the hammock's comfort. I shut my eyes and slept. When I woke up, I saw above me a hiker friend playing the ropes of the hammock like a bass. I laughed, and he smiled. Music can cure even the weariest of hearts.

As time passed and news from the injured hikers came in that no one was seriously hurt, it gave some room, some more clear air for a new balloon to inflate. The folks who remained at the inn enjoyed more music in the gazebo and a peaceful night's sleep. I left early Sunday morning to hitchhike back to where I got off the trail. A satellite TV guy, named Chad, gave me a ride. We stopped by his house and he gave me an energy drink and twenty bucks in trail magic. He wished me good luck as I made my way into the cow pasture that the trail meandered through for about a quarter of a mile. He is a good man, and I appreciate all the angels who helped us out along our journey.

I continued hiking on a fine Virginia morning. I saw some cows, and they mooed at me as I walked quickly through their country fresh air. Cow poop is "country fresh air," for the layman. The hike was a good hike into the evening. I wanted to get the twenty-one miles done before dark, so I was double-timing it to make it to the Tennessee–Virginia line. Completing one state on the AT is a pretty big deal (even the three miles of West Virginia), but in my mind knowing that I had just finished three states of the Appalachian Trail made me feel pretty stellar. To say I was proud to be alive when I hit the line at dark was an understatement.

With my headlamp illuminating the trail, the sign that said I had now entered Virginia was a sign of accomplishment. I continued down the trail with only a couple miles left until I arrived back in Damascus. My headlamp began to falter, but I continued hoping my eyes would adjust.

They didn't. Not fifty yards down the trail my foot hit a root and I began stumbling down the mountain path. It took several long strides to regain my balance, and thank my lucky stars there was not a rock garden for a trail out in front of my strides. I caught my breath and walked a few feet until I saw a light from a tent. I yelled out and explained my batteries had died in my headlamp and would they please let me borrow theirs while I set up my camping area not far away. They allowed me, and I got to work on setting my tent up next to some rocks that were once a fire pit.

I collected some kindling, some different-sized sticks, and a few dried logs and went to work on building a fire. Once I got it up and going, I gave back the headlamp that I had borrowed. The fire was warm and it lit up the inside of my tent. I laid back on top of my sleeping bag because the warmth from the fire and the temperature outside was not too bad and drifted off to sleep.

I woke up the next morning and quickly got my things together to hike into town. It was just a skip down the mountain and ridgeline. The town was quiet because Monday after Trail Days left only a few hikers who drank too much over the long, exciting weekend.

I hiked through the town where the AT markers were neatly displayed. It was neat crossing the old walking bridge and being a part of something larger than me. Humbled, I marched on through town until I met up with Honey Badger for breakfast/lunch with a few other hiking buds.

Polly and Rachel are two master hiking ladies whom I met somewhere in the Smokys, and that is what they were when they hiked past me . . . smoke. Polly and I lay on the grass at the end of town near a convenience store. We didn't talk all that much, just enjoyed the breeze and sunshine on our faces.

I stayed there for a lot longer than I wanted to, but I eventually forced myself toward the trail where it ran past a Subway restaurant. I grabbed an Italian hoagie and was on my way. A little bit more of a road walk before the trail crossed the highway and bolted up into the forested hillside outside of town.

Less than the mile up the trail, I made camp. It was a low mileage day, but knowing I got outside the city without staying another day was an accomplishment.

Once settled in, I heard the thunder. I took my tarp and made a roof above my pup tent. At this point, it was only shelter from the sun. Any dampness was going to get in. I was just happy I had an inflatable air mattress that allowed me to float a little bit, keeping the more important things like my phone and camera dry . . . er.

I fell asleep to the sound of thunder all around me; it lulled me to a nice bit of REM for the night. When I woke up, the sun was shining, and the puffy white clouds were all around as I stuck my head out of my tent. I quickly broke down camp and headed out up the mountain and across the ridgeline.

As soon as I hit the third ridgeline, the clouds opened up a torrential downpour. I had little time to grab my rain cover, and it was warm enough that I did not need my rain jacket. I walked for about fifteen solid minutes in the monsoon. My hands were pruning like raisins as I made it to the Virginia Creeper Trail where part of the AT had been washed out and closed from the super storm.

I walked the Creeper Trail for a good while. The rain subsided, and the sun was peeking out of the clouds. I saw a perfect rainbow, but only one and not a double like I have seen before in Fredericksburg. Several families and some other day touring folks on mountain bikes enjoyed the outdoors as they prescribed themselves up and down the well-graded trail.

The Appalachian Trail went off the Creeper Trail once for a mile or two and then went back again. As the Creeper Trail steadily climbed the mountain, there were several bridges with numbers on them to keep direction while riding or hiking. At a certain point, the Appalachian Trail cut off from the Creeper Trail for good and continued another steady climb to a shelter that was famous for the privy. I saw a hiker in the distance as I was heading up; as he approached, I noticed it was Nuke. I said hello, and he was not too happy. He commented that he was going to get off the trail and continue his music career. I wished him luck and continued to the shelter with the interesting privy.

The top of the mountain had a nice shelter, and I saw my friend, Roger, who had been hiking with me for some time. Roger was a retiree from Florida, and he completed some of the northern portions of the AT in New York. He told me about hiking through a zoo and walking across the Hudson River Bridge, which is somewhat of a highlight of the trail because one realizes the closeness of New York City. I liked Roger's insight. I had an Uncle Roger pass away from cancer. Talking to my hiking pal, Roger, made me think of the funny things Uncle Roger would say and do. He gave his condolences when I was explaining that everything happens for a reason, and I believe that my ancestors, including my uncle, were right there with me all along my journey. It felt good to say out loud, and I hope it was the case. During each day's hike, I wanted it to be the case. I think I mentioned to Roger my daily hiking goals, but several times we would hike together or near each other.

"I figured you were going to hike on farther today," Roger would say.

"I enjoy your company, I suppose," I answered.

The mountains resume going on forever along the fair trail system in Virginia's Iron Range. The weather was nice on the day I approached the Grayson Highlands, where hundreds of wild horses run free over the national park. Before I got there, I would see Roger for the last time before he climbed to the top of his namesake, Mount Rogers. The mountain was not on the AT, but it was the highest elevation mountain in Virginia. Sadly, I did not walk the side trail up to the summit; I continued on in the chilly breeze of the morning to take a short break at Thomas Knob Shelter and hiked on through the wild horses. There were about a dozen of them grazing around one of the many grassy balds. Someone snapped a quick picture as I continued to the Wise Shelter a few more miles away and subsequently five hundred AT miles complete. Did I feel like a badass? Uh, yes!

The shelter was full when I arrived, so I walked a dozen or so yards to set my tent up on a soft patch of grass next to my hiker pal, Critter. He and I built a fire, and as he was taking pictures of the full moon that night, I threw a log on the fire, sending sparks up into the air. I told him it was a pretty good shot when he showed it to me from his digital camera. With the wild horses behind me, I needed to rest for the next few days where I expected to get some bigger miles complete. Before heading off to bed, a cute couple weekend camping near us treated us to some delicious homemade goodies.

The next morning I hiked out into a fairly steady clip. My body at this point was feeling stronger, and I was beginning to increase the miles day to day. I hiked into some forest trail magic that had coolers, large Tupperware containers, a hiker entry journal, some chairs, and an umbrella. The foodstuffs were appreciated, and as I sat there with some other hikers in my mind, I wanted to stay for a longer time. I knew that I had to leave if I was going to continue to make it farther north and catch up to some of my original hiking family (also known as "tramily" Trail + Family = Tramily).

I had a pace of about three miles an hour the day I hiked into the much talked about Partnership Shelter run by the Mount Rogers information center. The shelter had two levels. There was a shower and a pizza delivery service. Some of my trail friends shared some of their leftover pizza they had gotten before I arrived. I walked to the Mount Roger's Visitor Center to charge my phone and make some phone calls.

Although I wanted to stay at the shelter, I knew that I had to continue up the trail to get resupplied in Atkins, Virginia. I motivated myself to say good-bye, but not before I let someone borrow my Esee knife. I realized ten miles down the trail I had left it with the person who borrowed it. I kicked myself for the error, but there was nothing I could do about it.

The highway was not far away as I made my way into Atkins, Virginia. The post office was a few miles from the trail, and I needed to get my resupply of food, batteries for my headlamp, toiletries, and other necessities. When I made a phone call to my cousin, she explained that she had sent a package to Troutdale, Virginia. This location was behind me now. Had I stayed at the Partnership Shelter, I would have been able to pick it up. Since I didn't, I immediately said good-bye to her and hitchhiked back to Troutdale. It took three hitches to get back. The second hitch was right at the Partnership Shelter, where my trail friend, B-Line, did an incredible job getting me a ride. He jumped up, hands clasped in prayer, when the truck pulled over. I yelled back to him as I ran to the truck, "Thanks, man! That was awesome!" He wished me luck, and I was off.

My last hitch took me to the post office. He said he would take me back to the trail where I got off when I retrieved my package, which was much relief to me. When I got out and approached the post office door, I noticed a note at eye level but paid little attention at first. I gripped the door and pulled hard. No go. It was locked! Dejected, I read the paper affixed to the door, new post office hours. I would have to stay. As I walked back to the car, a local man was doing some yard work on his property across the street from where we were. I asked him if he knew a good place to camp in the area. He explained to me that the church had a hostel only a mile up the road. The same church that put the coolers and chairs that were set up for hikers the day before. My kind ride dropped me off and said he would try to check on me in the morning to see if I had gotten a ride back out. Trail angels . . . I love them so much.

The church hostel was empty, and I did not see anyone from the time I arrived to the time I left the next morning. They had a donation can and I threw in a few bucks for my stay. I got an early start, and while I was walking and hitching, it was only fifteen minutes until a guy from my home state and a section hiker I had met less than a week prior pulled over and said, "Uke?" Awesome! He was Johnny-on-the-spot. He gave me a ride back to Atkins, where he and I ate at the Barn Restaurant and talked about trail stuff. He was very kind, and he gave me his number for when I arrived in Pennsylvania at his home. I said my good-byes and hiked under the bridge of Interstate 81. The trail curved and began a steady climb. A fellow thru-hiker, named Tennessee, was full bearded like me, and we hiked the next hundred miles or so together to Pearisburg, Virginia.

Whistling. Lots and lots of whistling. That is what happens on the trail. Then you sing, "Whistle while you work . . . da da Da da da Da Da!"

Tennessee got a room in Pearisburg, and I took a shower and decided that I was going to continue hiking. We both decided to get some all-you-can-eat Chinese food before parting. The restaurant on the opposite side of the street from the hotel was unremarkable, and the fare was less than stellar, but the caloric intake was what I craved.

We went back to the hotel. I thanked him for allowing me to use his room, and we said our good-byes.

Chapter Seven

The hike out of Pearisburg was interesting. The mountain loomed in the distance as I hiked on concrete for a few miles before hitting the dirt path again. It was a big uphill climb into the Rice Field Shelter. As I was making my way up, I could hear a howl behind me, "Uuuke!?" It was Yote (a.k.a. Neil) and I was happy to see him as he caught right up with me.

He and I hiked into the top of mountain where the Rice Field Shelter was located. We settled in as we overlooked the cities in the distance. It was calm and serene with a bit of sharp wind cruising into the front of the shelter. We had some small talk as we ate our dinner.

"There is a trail festival in Troutdale, Virginia, in three days," Yote explained.

"How far are we from here?" I asked.

"Fifty miles. If we can hike twenty-five each day, we can get there pretty easily."

"I'm in. Let's get some rest and get up early in the a.m. to crush out some miles."

The next morning we were a little slow moving, but in good spirits to begin our day. Midmorning we were clipping along the Appalachian Trail like a couple of schoolboys headed to the one-room schoolhouse during the nineteenth century. It was pretty cool. The sky was partly cloudy with the sun warming us as we climbed over an open field and into the thick pine forest ahead.

We came to Pine Swamp Branch Shelter where Hightide and Blockade Runner were eating their lunch. The four of us talked a while. I told them our fifty-mile plan to get to the trail fest and they were supportive. We gave hugs and hiked out.

We stopped for lunch at Bailey Gap Shelter and made some lunch in a gallon ziplock baggy. After we ate all of the contents, we decided to take a rest. We both napped a bit just as a rainstorm passed over our sheltered heads.

"That was good timing!" Yote exclaimed.

We camped at War Spur Shelter and the next day hiked again in a soft sprinkle before the clouds moved out and the sun gleamed overhead. We were moving well before descending from Johns Creek Mountain. At Kelly Knob we decided to take a bathroom break and a quick breather. I sat down on a rotten log and felt a small prick on my right leg. I swatted what I thought was a twig. I felt the same prick on my buttocks and again swatted the "twig" away.

The trail was gradual and kind. I saw a deer pouncing through the forest about thirty yards from where I hiked. As the path veered downhill, it opened into yet another field. We saw a plethora of cows grazing on the luscious grasses. We arrived at the road crossing just before the famous oak tree that towers above like a beacon in the sky.

Yote and I stopped at the tree and took some pictures of ourselves by the massive Keffer Oak. After taking it all in, we donned our packs again and began hiking. Less than a hundred feet up the trail, my eyes started to defeat me. The grass was growing quickly and squirming like a snake trying to get away from a predator. I looked around, squinted hard, and then looked at the trees doing the same thing. Something was very wrong.

"What's wrong?" Yote asked as I lay in the thick grass to the edge of the trail.

"Not sure, but I'm hallucinating."

I got up and continued up into the mountain, hoping the movement would cure what was ailing me. I made light of the situation and made a few jokes while my body would only allow me less than two miles per hour. Yote was concerned, but supportive. I drank all of my water and most of his. We were less than a mile away from the next shelter that we were not planning on stopping at. The shelter was almost a half-mile off of the AT, but it was switched back at almost a vertical drop.

"I have to stop. You can keep going, and I can catch up if you want," I said.

"No, I can stop with you. Are you all right?" Yote asked, concerned.

"I am not sure. But I feel different."

"Let's get down to the shelter, get some water, and discuss our plan."

"Okay."

I walked gingerly down to the Sarver Hollow Shelter. The clouds and fog rolled in slowly. The visibility was less than ten feet in front of us. It took what seemed like forever to find the shelter. Yote called out that he had found it, and I followed his voice.

He was looking for the sign that explained how to get to the water source for the shelter.

"It is pretty far away."

"I can wait until the morning. I just need to rest."

Clumsily, I prepared my bed, grabbed my food bag, and took out three pieces of turkey jerky. I chewed and almost choked on the small amount of food in my mouth. Then I took out three ibuprofen and two Benadryl, popped them in my mouth, and went to sleep.

I woke up in the middle of the night with cotton mouth and no water. There were a few drops in my water bottle that helped a little, and I went back to sleep. During the night, I woke up several times in different positions around the huge expanse of the shelter floor. Luckily it was only him and me in the structure, or I would have upset a lot of people.

The next morning the rain was coming down in sheets. A literal torrential downpour.

"I'm going to get us some water," Yote said as he grabbed my water pouch and headed out into the storm.

"Thanks!" I yelled back.

I felt something on my leg, and it was painful. I lifted my camp shorts and uncovered a huge goiter. I felt again, and I had two huge bumps on my left leg. I thought back to the log and the "twigs." At that moment I realized they may not have been twigs.

Yote arrived back with four liters of water and about three liters dripping off of him.

"I'm not going anywhere anytime soon." As I said this, I showed him the bumps.

"Holy shit! That is not okay."

"Thanks. I need to drink a lot of water. Then I need to eat. I will see how I feel afterward. What are you going to do?"

"I'll stay with you."

I felt sorry that I may have been holding him up and a feeling of gratitude that he would want to make sure I was safe. Knowing that if he did leave I would be by myself made me feel a little nervous. But I had made it this far; I was not going to give up because of a couple of red goiters on my leg.

"It is possible no one is coming to the shelter. The rain has not let up all morning."

"I know, and when people arrive at the sign for this shelter, they'll see not only is it nearly a half mile off-trail, it is entirely downhill. Holy shit, we are going to have to climb that shit when we leave."

"Yep."

After eating and drinking about a liter and a half of water, I lay down and went to sleep. A few hours later, I was waked by the sounds of Polly coming into the shelter. She was a sight for sore eyes. Soaked to the gills, but smiling brightly because that is just who she is.

"Hi! I didn't think anyone would be here," she said.

"We wouldn't have been, but Uke had something bite him," Yote replied.

I showed Polly my goiters and tried to give some comedy to an otherwise poopy situation. She was pretty sure it was a spider of some kind and that I would probably need to get to a hospital right away. I thanked her for her assessment when Blockade Runner and Hightide rolled in along with Guardian and Angel.

There were great people who all gave me suggestions as to what the hell was happening on my leg. I knew Hightide was a nurse, so I was very happy to see her. I showed her and explained what I thought had happened. She agreed that it was a bite and that it may heal on its own. She also offered that it would be a good idea to get off the trail and get it looked at by a doctor in the next town.

I had a few options. I could go south and return to the road or continue thirty miles. After my nap, I explained that I would be zeroing in this shelter as the rains were not letting up. Several other people arrived, and we had a full house. Everyone offered their support and encouragement for me. I was grateful I had the knowledge of so many gifted people around me during this stressful time.

Evening came and the rains subsided. Sleep was difficult for me, but I did get the rest I needed to continue north for the next hike. I was confident I could make it, goiters and all.

Yote and I were the last ones out of the shelter. We hiked up the mountain to the trailhead where we left off two days prior. I was disappointed I did not accomplish the goal of getting to the trail festival, but I knew my health was more important.

Another trail friend gave me a painkiller to help with the pain and get me rocking and a-rolling.

It was a somewhat difficult hike, and as we passed the first shelter, I had caught up with two hiking friends I hadn't seen in a long while. First Gear and Greenlite were kicking some AT ass. I knew, with my new circumstances, I may never see them again.

Yote and I continued on and made it to the Pickle Branch Shelter before the Dragon's Tooth. The Dragon's Tooth is a famous rock outcropping in the mountain that resembles, yep, you guessed it, a dragon's tooth. There were several people at the shelter eating lunch or munching on some snacks. Someone had peanut M&M's and dropped one.

"Are you going to eat that?" Polly asked, eyeing the single M&M on the ground.

"No."

Polly picked it up, blew some dirt off of it, and popped it in her mouth. There are several sayings that go around to separate the kinds of hikers out there. "If a morsel of food is on the ground, what do the three types of hikers do when they see it? A weekender hiker will step on it, a section hiker will step over it, and a thru-hiker will pick it up and eat it." The cravings for calories are a real thing out in the wilderness. I have never heard of anyone getting sick from doing such things, more so from not purifying water. Me? I purify about 25 percent of the time on the trail. If I am at the top of a mountain and a spring is flowing with crystal clear goodness, I raw dog that deliciousness like eating a turkey leg.

My leg goiters were getting bigger and I could see the redness spreading. They were becoming rounder and rounder. I sat down at the shelter and thought out my next plan. Yote was moving on. I really wanted to go on, but I was given sound advice to stay put, rest, and drink plenty of fluids before tackling the next fifteen miles. I chose that option due to the variables that lie ahead.

The steep ups and downs in the next leg were an issue. I needed to gain some energy. During dinner there was laughter and an upbeat attitude amongst all of the hikers. The shelter was much smaller and we were cramped in pretty tight. There was no chance of me rolling around on this shelter floor unless I rolled over people.

Sleep came, and I enjoyed it. I was not up super early, and again I was one of the last folks out of the shelter the next a.m. Breakfast and the donning of my pack and I was out. The trail swooped and dropped over rocks and roots. The weather cooperated, and I made it just as the sign for the Dragons' Tooth came into view. It was so close I could smell it. But I knew that I needed to be somewhere safe and make decisions on my next moves along this wild and crazy adventure.

Another thru-hiker, named Bon Air, saw that I was struggling over the rock edge of the Dragon's back.

"Are you all right?"

"No, not really." I pulled up my pant leg to show him one of my goiters.

"Oh, that does not look good. Are you going to the hospital?" he asked, concerned.

"I think so, yes."

"I think you should get to the ER as soon as possible."

"I'll hike with you for a while."

Bon Air walked with me until the tenth of a mile side trail led to the Dragon's Tooth. He wished me luck, and I was thankful he pushed me those miles to get out of the wilderness safely. Had it not been for him, I would have still made it, but much more slowly.

There would be times I would wear my grumpy pants. Like when I saw people drinking good beer. If they were drinking lite beer and I was drinking water, I felt fine about that. I mean, we were practically drinking the same thing. Hiking to beer was my mission, and by God if I was going to let some spider ruin it for me. It was watching the folks drinking the exquisite, hoppy loveliness that got my panties all in a bunch.

The Dragon's Tooth hiking area was pretty full because it was a weekend. People waited to climb the rock faces as I was stumbling my way down the mountain. I got to the road, and a nice couple gave me a ride to the Four Pines Hostel. In my opinion, it is the best hostel in the southern Appalachia. Joe and his son, Joe, greeted me when I arrived.

Several hikers who were there had already heard of my plight and were wondering when I was going to go to the hospital. I talked to Joe, and he said any time I was ready to go he would take me. The kindness was overwhelming. I did take some time looking over my goiters and listened to advice from others. Some offered to knife them open. But more sound advice came from Hightide. She said if I didn't have a fever, then I may be able to wait to get checked up after the weekend was over.

I agreed to wait it out. In a start, I woke up. My head was pounding. I took my temperature; it was 104. I thought to myself, "That's not okay."

I walked out to where Joe and some other hikers were playing cornhole.

"Joe, would you mind taking me to the ER?"

"Not at all. Let's go," he said compassionately.

Just like that, we were on our way. Me, Joe, and his son made it to the emergency room in no time at all. As I walked to the front desk to check in, I lifted my shorts to show the receptionist, and just as I lifted over the first goiter . . . POP!

"Whoa, hold on a minute," the receptionist said as he scampered through the door behind him. Less than minute later, he came out and said, "Have a seat and someone will be with you soon."

My goiter had spit out and popped like a huge zit on my leg, revealing puss and overall disgustingness right in front of the ER receptionist. I guess that was lucky because I didn't wait all that long to get in to see the doctor.

The nurse took my vitals. I sat and waited for someone to tell me what I needed to do so I could continue my hike. My doctor was an attractive female, and she was very helpful. Although she was not thoroughly familiar with the procedure, she was calm and truthful.

"I'm going to have to read up on this and how to treat it. Sit tight. I'll be back."

"Okay, do you think it was a spider?"

"It very well could have been, but unless you saw it, we are not 100 percent on that. I'll be right back."

"K."

I was fairly calm about everything. The nurse came in, drew blood, and looked at my goiter. The goiter on my ass was not visible, but I kept the one on my leg open to watch. It was pulsating a bit. I asked the nurse to take my picture as the needle was in my arm. She did. It was quite the shot.

They prepped me for the lancing. The doctor put enough Novocain in both goiters to bring down a small horse. She explained what she had to do and that I probably wouldn't feel anything with the amount of "local" she put in. I understood and only had one question.

"Can I video this?"

"Um . . . that is against policy here."

"I promise only to use it for educational purposes."

"Ah, well, I guess that would be okay. Yes you can. Do you want me to? I could probably get a better angle?" the nurse asked.

"That'd be great," I said enthusiastically.

The nurse recorded with my phone while my doctor took out a steak knife and eye protection. Just kidding. It was an X-Acto knife and a visor.

"I don't want to be sprayed."

"Will it spray all over?" I asked.

"I am not sure what is going to happen."

"That is reassuring."

She then put on the antibacterial medicine around both goiters and started with my leg first. When she sliced it open, it did spray a little. First puss and bile and just evil poured out of my leg. I watched the nurse put her hand over her mouth and gasp. The doctor then began squeezing the evil out, and it was a lot! A lot a lot of poison came out of my first goiter. It was the smaller of the goiters, and I was a bit nervous for my ass goiter. My doc then took a pair of scissors and poked and prodded through my open wound in my leg. I felt it, first just the initial movement, and then I felt her hit a nerve, and that was painful.

"Ahh!" I gasped in pain.

"Sorry," she said as she continued the process of poking, pulling, and squeezing.

"I need to be sure I am getting it all out."

"I know."

Then I began singing a song, making the situation more bearable for everyone in the room. Other hospital staff came in and had the same reaction as my nurse. The doc put a string of cloth with the antibacterial medicine of some sort deep down into my wound. She repeated the process after bandaging my leg on my ass.

After it was all done, I went out to Joe and his son to leave. We got into his truck, and I pulled up the video on my phone. The video was disgusting, but pure gold. Joe asked if I had to return to the hospital, and I told him I did have to go back for a checkup in two days. He said I was more than welcome to stay at the hostel while I healed.

During my eight-day stay at Four Pines, I received so much love and support from my friends and family in the form of messages, calls, cards, and packages. Alpine, the girl I met on my first day out on the trail, came to the hostel with a burger, fries, and pop.

She had her car, and we drove into Daleville, Virginia, to visit some of my hiker trash friends, including Yote, who was also concerned about me. The love I felt was huge. I can't thank the Four Pines Hostel, my friends, and family enough for the kind thoughts during this severe setback.

Many people thought that I would quit and go back home. Those people didn't hear very well when I told them I gave up beer to accomplish this goal. Giving up was not an option; I love beer way too much. Others were the complete opposite; they knew I was going to continue and do my best to make it to Maine. No pain, no rain, no Maine.

I did my best to help out around the hostel by mowing the lawn and keeping the place neat and tidy for the next set of hikers. Many hikers came and went; it was very disconcerting, but the company and uplifting well-wishes kept me focused on my objectives.

Joe drove the hikers who wanted to eat at the Home Place, one of the most famous AT buffets on the trail, for a small donation. During my stay, I ate there twice, and the fixings that this restaurant threw down were well worth the stop. I opted primarily for the two meat options: ham and fried chicken. The homemade goodness was delectable.

And they kept the servings coming. And if one could not finish their last full plate, a to-go container was provided. If you are ever in the Catawba, Virginia, area, I highly recommend eating there.

The night before I was planning to hike back out, some of my hiker trash friends had a bonfire. The Sun Gods were there, and I was starting to feel better. We did a lot of chiding each other in fun. They partied like rock stars and were content in their reverie.

My friend, Chris, whom I met on hell day in the Muskrat Creek Shelter, was around the fire. One of the Sun Gods asked him his trail name.

"Steve," Chris said sarcastically.

"You're name is Steve?"

"No, it's Chris."

Bellyfuls of laughter ensued, and then and there Chris received his trail name, "Scuba Steve." Scuba Steve waited for me and hiked my trail seven miles to see how my leg wounds would hold up. I said my good-byes and gave my appreciation to the Four Pines Hostel. Scuba and I hiked out gradually and made it to our destination before the evening. I cared for my wounds, ate some dinner, and went to bed.

A milestone for me the next day was Scuba Steve and I arriving at one of the most pictured places on the Appalachian Trail: MacAfee's Knob. The day was overcast but pleasant. We stayed for about an hour, taking in the rock ledge that jettisoned out about fifteen yards over the expanse of the mountain. It was a brilliant site. He and I snapped a few pictures before moving on our way.

Less than two miles from MacAfee was Tinker Cliffs, and the area was just as cool, if not cooler, than McAfee—much less traffic and in many ways a better view, but don't tell anyone; let it be our little secret.

During this trip, I was making a consistent goal of signing all of the trail registries. Ninety-nine percent of all the shelters had them. In trail towns, many businesses also had registries for hikers to sign. What this did was establish a line of communication with other hikers. The hikers sign this register in one of the several ways. The most basic is just to sign it with a trail name. Some notes were written to warn people of possible dangers in the area (snakes, mice, bear, bobcat, coyotes, woolly mammoth, and the occasion Big Foot sighting). Other hikers would write a Bible passage, some would draw an elaborate portrait of the surrounding area, and unbelievably often people would write in them of a gear item they left behind at another shelter/area and their phone number to get it returned. Nine times out of ten, the item would be returned to them. And that is how the trail community works. People helping people get through the act of life, life worth the effort.

Scuba Steve would always sign by using Adam Sandler's character in Big Daddy, Scuba Steve's tagline, which went something like, "Scuba Steve says make sure you drink plenty of water." He had some more silly ones throughout our journey together, but I am writing most of this by the seat of my pants. Entertaining enough? If not, it gets better. Maaaaybe.

Chapter EIGHT

Scuba Steve and I left each other somewhere near a babbling brook and a wooden walking bridge. We had camped out right next to the stream. After building a fire and talking for a bit, we went to bed. The next morning I was up around six and began the ritual of packing up and cooking my breakfast. I yelled over to him and asked him if he was getting up. He said he wanted to sleep some more and that he would catch up with me. The two holes in my leg were healing up nicely from my body being in constant rhythm with nature.

When I was working at the group home near Washington, DC, I was thinking of the kids I was counseling. A few of them liked to fish. Me being from Pennsylvania, fishing is in my DNA, thanks in part to my father teaching me at a young age. I was able to teach some of what I picked up throughout my life.

One particular day I took four of the kids to the Potomac River to catch some catfish. I have taught some friends in Virginia about how catfish love eel. A circle hook with an inch of eel flesh will draw a catfish in almost always. Several clients I had out fishing that day never fished a day in their lives. I'll never forget when the line pulled on him as he reeled in a two-pound catfish. His face lit up in a smile, and it was a happy moment in an otherwise stressful life for him. He asked if we were going to be able to eat the fish. Why stop with the life lesson there? So I made some calls and got permission to teach the client how to filet and cook up a fish. He was not allowed to handle a knife, and there were other strict rules for the clients in the group home that I needed to adhere to.

When I brought the group of boys back to campus, I pulled the young man who had caught the fish to the side.

"When the community group and evening chores get done, I'll take you out and show you how to filet the fish you caught. Then we'll cook him up with some butter and onion."

"Okay! Thanks, Mr. Lloyd," he said as a smile ran ear to ear.

He could not wait to show off his fish. I kept my word and did as I said I would do. I gave him the option to eat the fish himself or share with his peers. It was a test, and he did not disappoint. Several of the clients were interested in eating the fish that wafted a delicious smell throughout the home. He shared that fish and created a positive rapport amongst his peers. These and other stories, at times not so pleasant, were running through my mind as I hiked.

My thoughts on this and other positive work situations came to a halt when I came to the town of Daleville, Virginia. The sky had been mostly sunny for the day, but when I crossed over the highway, some rain clouds looked to be moving in. I made a quick stop at the gas station and spoke to a trail friend who was grabbing something before heading back to her motel room. We talked for a few minutes, and then said our good-byes.

The next small section hike into the town of Troutville was a reward. Hikers have an opportunity to do laundry and shower at the fire station a short distance up the road from the trail. I made my way there to shower and wash my stinky clothes. When I completed, I returned to the trail, where Scuba Steve and I camped by the AT sign. I put my tent up in the misting rain, ate a quick dinner, and went to sleep.

I was a bit wet when I woke up the next morning from some condensation on the tent walls. I quickly packed up and began walking back to town. The grocery store was open, and I took advantage by getting a bunch of fresh fruits and veggies to hike into the next shelter as a bit of trail magic for whoever showed up.

The hike from Troutville to Fullhardt Knob Shelter was mainly uphill. The trail was somewhat muddy from the day before, but I kept my footing as I walked from the farming hills and into the mountain forest.

Once I arrived at the shelter, I waited for Scuba Steve. He arrived, and we made a plan to night hike out and try to accomplish some big miles. I made a sort of fruit salad, and Peach Tree came. Peach Tree was from Missouri, and he was a hell of a guy. He lost his father and was carrying some of his ashes with him around his neck. He and I would come to know each other more through Pennsylvania and New Jersey, where we had some pretty stellar experiences.

Scuba Steve and I were discussing and reminiscing on the Grayson Highlands and the wild horses. He was telling me a story about a girl whom he met by fear. The horses were a bit temperamental the day Jo Cool and Scuba Steve happened to be there. These wild animals were apparently being fed by tourists and wanted food from this girl. One of the horses began nipping and biting at her. She started to run down the rocky terrain of the trail, but the horse was unrelenting. She ran screaming to Scuba Steve. He turned and saved her from the wild beast with some grunts and growls and maybe a few pats on the fanny. After he had told this story, we all had a laugh and then, out of coincidence perhaps, the girl arrived at Fullhardt Shelter. She was like an apparition.

I had heard of her before. She was an incredible singer and also enjoyed playing the ukulele. Scuba Steve couldn't hide his astonishment that he had just got done telling the story of the girl he saved over 230 miles away from where we now sat. He hadn't seen her since. It was somewhat odd, to say the least.

"You didn't believe me, did you?" Scuba Steve asked.

"Um, yeah, yeah I believed you," I replied.

"No you didn't," Scuba Steve laughed.

"Well it's true, and here I am. He did save me from that bad pony," Jo Cool chimed in.

Jo Cool sat with the three of us in the shelter and asked what our plans were. We already had Peach Tree on board for the night hike. When we told Jo Cool, she was on board, as well. So the four of us rested and slept as best we could for the good twenty miles or more night hike we were planning.

"Good night, John boy," I said as I put down my head.

I woke to the sound of pots clanking. The plan was to start moving around nine, prepare our meals, pack up, don headlamps, and be hiking by ten p.m. We were moving somewhat slowly, but as we began to get some caloric intake, we were a bit more peppy.

We had a small fire going in the fire pit when three headlamps approached our late dinner in the shelter. It was obvious when they came into the shelter that they planned to sleep there. Jo Cool suggested we move our things to the picnic table so they could get settled in after hiking a long day.

The packing up was tedious, and I was checking and double-checking to make sure I hadn't forgotten anything. Once we were all ready, we formed a line, with me at the front for pace. Once we got moving, our bodies warmed up and we were running pretty well through the Virginia forest. It was very dark, and when I would hit a switchback, I would yell, "Switchback! Thanks a lot, Bob." To say our foursome was anything but jovial would be a complete understatement.

The trail crossed a pretty good stream, and we could hear the rushing water as we made our way down the mountain trail. The sound got louder and louder the closer we approached. A hammock was mere feet away from the trail as we arrived at the rich stream. All of us filled up with water and heard the hammock talk. We were pretty loud rolling through the forest, and we all felt bad for waking this great guy up.

"Hi, sorry that we were so loud," Jo Cool said.

"Oh, it's no problem. Where are all of you headed?" he asked.

"Trying to get big miles out tonight, and we are loud to inform the bears that we're here," I laughed.

"Oh, I don't think anything is going to be bothering you guys." He chuckled.

"Ain't nobody got no time for any of that," I sang.

We filled up on water, ate some snacks, and donned packs to begin our hike again.

Sometimes we walked in silence because we still felt somewhat sorry that we could be waking up our fellow hikers. But when Jo Cool began singing, we were all in a rhythm that made us all forget any pain we may be experiencing. She sang a few songs and sometimes I would chime in with her if I knew the words to what she was singing or I would just adlib a bit. The one song that kept us moving at a good pace she sang was by Josh Ritter called, "To the Dogs or Whoever."

The four of us came to a shelter, and many people were sleeping, but we wanted to check the log to see who signed it ahead of us. So we moseyed into Wilson Creek Shelter. I quietly grabbed the logbook, opened it, and the first names I saw I recognized. Then I got kind of loud and said, "Do you guys know Chuckles and Lil Spoon? They signed in here today! I thought they were so far ahead of us," I said excitedly. They didn't know them, but some movement came from inside the shelter.

"Hey, do you guys know how far Chuckles and Lil Spoon were trying to get today?" I asked.

The female voice replied, "We are Chuckles and Lil Spoon."

"No Shit!" I responded for the rest of camp to hear me.

I thought they had still been off the trail for a wedding they were attending. We talked for a while. I tried to convince them to come with us. They declined. The comedy was there. Steady Eddie was in the shelter with them and said hello and "Shut the fuck up." Something to that effect.

We said our good-byes and made our way to the first crossing of the Blue Ridge Parkway, Skyline Drive. It's fucking famous! All of us decided to take it all in the distance we had all traversed from Georgia. To this point we had hiked 741 miles from the beginning. "Started from the bottom, now we're here" was the great indicator. The stars were amazingly bright, and our spirits were surprisingly high. We all breathed deeply, donned our packs once again, and headed the first of several dozen crossings of the BRP that lay ahead.

As I continued to lead, I felt something happening on my inner thighs. "Oh shit," I thought aloud.

"What's wrong?" Scuba Steve asked.

"I'm chaffing, and it is gonna be bad," I said.

"Are you going to be able to make it?"

"I'll stop at the next shelter and see how I feel."

Jo Cool continued to honor us with her voice as we made our way to the beautiful, yet dark, trail junction sign for Bobletts Gap Shelter.

The shelter was full when we arrived. We did our business, retrieved some water, and I made my decision to rest my very painful thighs a while at the shelter. Jo Cool, Scuba Steve, and Peach Tree moved on while I got out some Vitamin I (Ibruprofen) and waited for someone from the shelter to hike out so I could take their place. We wished each other luck and said our "See ya soon." I could hear Jo Cool singing as they made their way back up to the trail. A spot opened up not long after Jo Cool, Scuba Steve, and Peach Tree left. I put some ointment on my sore, hot thighs, threw my sleeping bag down, and fell fast asleep.

When I woke up, Chuckles and Lil Spoon greeted me with smiles and questioned why I was down in the shelter. I explained my unfortunate predicament and they laughed some more. I woke up and hit the privy and began packing up to hike a bit more.

Chuckles and Lil Spoon didn't stop long and were on their way before I donned my pack and made my way back to the trail.

My hiking speed was slow as I crossed Bearwallow Gap and a neat little footbridge. When I started the ascent up Cove Mountain, dark clouds began curling in from every- where around me. I knew if I did not speed up, I was going to be in a hell of a storm. Lucky for me the trail was forgiving while I began running up the mountain.

Summiting over both Cove and Little Cove Mountains was surprisingly easy. Then the descent down into the Cove Mountain Shelter is where the moisture began in a trickle. I was less than a hundred yards from the shelter when the droplets became drops. I peered inside to find Steady Eddie, Chuckles, Lil Spoon, and a mother/son section hiker team sleeping in the shelter.

I tried to keep the inside of the shelter dry by getting out of my wet boots and clothes before climbing into the dry pad to change into my warm, dry camp clothes. We talked about trail stories past, and I wondered how far Peach Tree, Jo Cool, and Scuba Steve had gotten before making their camp.

Cove Mountain was home for the night until the next morning's rituals. The weather was a bit better, and the sun seemed to want to come out for the visit. Research of the next thirty miles showed several steep ups and downs. Steady Eddie and I made a tentative goal to hike from Cove Mountain Shelter to Matt's Creek Shelter, which was about twenty-nine miles. The guidebook said there was a swimming hole not far away, and we were all pretty excited to jump in. Steady Eddie and I were the first ones in, and we bathed a bit of our stink off as we swam in Jenny's Creek. The sun came out strong, and it was an exciting summer day in Virginia.

After we had left the creek, my body temperature was lower. I believe if we did not jump into the river, then that next climb would have been much more challenging. First up was a thousand foot climb and over Fork Mountain. We swept it up pretty quickly. Then myself, Steady, and the young section hiker began a nice steady run down into another taj-ma-shelter, called Bryant Ridge Shelter. This shelter had a large sitting area and enough sleeping areas for twenty hikers to sleep comfortably. It was two-floor structure and had a beautiful area to break for lunch.

We were all pretty sweaty, so we got out of our shirts to put them in the sun while we rested and ate. I notice a few honeybees had gathered on our shirts as they dried. A few turned into ten, then twenty, and then so many bees that I could not count them all. They didn't bother me, but I noticed Steady swiping them away. I suggested he leave them be, and he agreed.

When we prepared to leave, I grabbed my bee-covered shirt and calmly swung it back and forth until they were all off. Some of them had gathered inside my shirt, so I turned it inside out, and those bees flew away when I shook it again. I noticed Steady did the same, but he did not turn his shirt inside out before he put it on. Once he put his shirt on, I heard him yell and curse. Steady Eddie ran away from the area and was outraged. I asked him if he was allergic and he said he was not. We donned our packs again and headed up yet another big climb. The 1,800 foot ascent up to Floyd Mountain was a steep hike. When we finished, we were pretty happy with ourselves.

We passed on the Cornelius Creek Shelter by just stopping for a short break before heading back out. The hike up to Apple Orchard Falls Trail gave some incredible views of the skyline and an enormous building that housed the Federal Aviation Administration tower. Steady and I stopped to enjoy the picturesque view until we hiked onto Thunder Hill Shelter.

Here, a trail friend was doing some trail magic by way of making it a game for hikers. He brought beer—ugh—and several snacks for his other hiker friends. The Thunder Hill Shelter was right off of the Blue Ridge Parkway, so getting trail magic in for hikers was a breeze. It was sweet of him to give not only of his time but his snacks.

My feet were yelling at me as we rested and talked about our plan. I took my boots off and saw why they were so sore. Dishpan hands suck, but dishpan feet? Suck worse. I put some powder on my feet and told Steady Eddie I wasn't sure if I was going to make it. He agreed to stay at the shelter and get to Glasgow, Virginia, the next day.

Steady and I hiked out the next morning at a good pace and made it to Matt's Creek Shelter to break for a very short time. The black flies there were unforgiving. These little gnats drew blood for each bite and both Steady and I had few blood drops on our arms, legs, and backs. We quickly hiked along the James River for about a mile before arriving at the longest foot-use-only bridge on the Appalachian Trail.

The James River footbridge was an old CSX railroad bridge. A trail enthusiast, named Bill Foot, began the idea of the project. Hikers who have crossed this incredible expanse are grateful he did.

Steady and I approached the bridge crossing, and the first thing we saw before walking up the steps was a diamondback rattlesnake sitting right in our path. The snake was curled and ready to strike as we tried to walk around the dangerous reptile. I took a few pebbles and threw them in front of it to alert it. I didn't want to hurt the poor guy. Steady tossed a rock and hit it on his backside. The snake slithered away so we could continue our walk across.

The weather was great as we approached a parking area. Highway 501 was very busy, and it is hard to cross. When we got to the parking area, several outfitter busses were there shuttling kayakers. We approached one of the drivers to ask if we could get a ride into Glasgow. He had to ask the group leader if they minded. The manager did not care, and we got our ride into town.

Glasgow, Virginia, is a small trail and adventure community that is very supportive of adventurers. Steady and I thanked our ride and walked over to a local Italian restaurant to get some grub before checking out the town shelter there.

During our meal, I realized I had left all of my notes and my journal in the shuttle. For the life of me, I could not think of where the shuttle service hailed from. Losing my notes for the past 780 miles was more than discouraging. My only thought was I hope I was able to recall the pertinent information to be able to rewrite it later on.

The Glasgow town shelter was well equipped with a privy, hot showers, and a pretty stellar fire pit. Several hikers were there rebooting from some injuries and other trail happenstances. It was nice to hang out around the fire and have some laughs. Trail comedy is uplifting and refreshing for sore, worn-out bodies.

Steady and I were out and back on the trail midmorning. We got a quick ride back to the parking area where a trail legend was doing trail magic. A longtime hiker, by the trail name Santa's Little Helper, was giving out drinks and snacks. We shared condition trail talk and the trail telephone of asking of other hiker friends' whereabouts. We bid Santa's Little Helper good-bye and thanked him for his kindness.

The goal for the day was a twenty-mile hike into Brown Mountain Creek Shelter. It was a gorgeous day for it. The sun was shining through the trees, and the trail was forgiving under our feet. I signed the trail journal at Johns Hollow Shelter and got back to hiking right away. There were several excellent views over Little and Big Rocky Row. Then we hiked some ridge walking over Saddle and Salt Log Gaps. The climb up Bluff Mountain was enjoyable, but hard.

Bluff Mountain has a monument erected for a young boy barely five years old who died there in the year 1890. This young boy got lost while out gathering firewood. He was seven miles from where he walked off from Tower Hill Schoolhouse in Amherst County, Virginia. Rest in peace, Ottie Cline Powell. The young soul will forever roam the Blue Ridge.

Chuckles, Lil Spoon, Steady, and I discussed heading into Buena Vista, Virginia. We made tentative plans as we continued to hike down to Punchbowl Mountain and Shelter. We went to an impressive overlook and sat there in reverence. Once we arrived at the first road heading into Buena Vista, we decided to continue the original goal of getting into Brown Mountain Creek Shelter.

We all came to the shelter just before nightfall. The privy was the spawn of the devil. The smells were so bad that I began hacking up before even opening the door. But I did my business and only puked a little bit. Once we settled in after eating and preparing our beds, it did not take long for us to be sleeping soundly.

Steady Eddie decided to go into Buena Vista. We said our good-byes and good lucks. Peach Tree and I met up again. I mentally prepared for the 2,700-foot climb of Bald Knob. I was not doing the twenty-seven-to-ten counts as much, but I did need a consistent push of a loud "Ya Ta Hay!" up the huge mountain. I got that hiking cadence from my friend Chief-Hike-A-Trail. He was from out west and was very fun to be around. Every time I would see him, he would chant out loudly, "Ya Ta Hay!" The song worked for me getting up to the top of Bald Knob. Although called "Bald," it was very much below the tree line.

As I reached the top, I was sweating like a stuck pig. I grabbed my phone to get in touch with an old friend from high school. She agreed to take my hiker trash self in so I could get laundered and cleaned up. We decided on a meet up at the Tye River Suspension Bridge. I was about twenty-one miles away and told her I would be there the next morning.

There was a slight descent into Cow Camp Gap Shelter, where Peach Tree and I took a breather. That was a steady fun hike over Cole Mountain, down to Hog Camp Gap, up again to Tar Jacket Ridge, and down again to Salt Log Gap. The view from Salt Log Gap was of the Blue Ridge Mountains spreading for miles in rolling mountain wonder.

I wanted to get to The Priest Shelter, but when we arrived at the Steeley-Woodworth Shelter, my knee popped out of socket as I was taking a snack break at the picnic table. I have had knee issues for years, and I contributed the injury to both getting old and playing football as a kid.

The group of hikers at the shelter were concerned as I struggled to get my knee back into place. It was very painful. Pushing and pulling my leg was not working. I stopped messing with it and sat still for about twenty minutes. After about thirty minutes, I finally was able to get it back in place and walk. I wasted too much time; the sun was going down, so I decided to call it a night in the shelter.

There was no one awake the next morning when I headed out. I tested my knee a bit before kicking it into high gear to make the meet up with Sarah at the Tye River Suspension Bridge. The hike there took me close to Spy Rock camping area. The area had huge boulders all around and hiking scrambles up their face. What the glaciers moved and the way they folded the mountains were quite impressive to my eye.

There were several day hikers walking in the area around the Priest Mountain parked at the Crabtree Falls Campground. A woman and her two friends asked to get their picture taken with me before I hiked to the summit of The Priest Mountain. If I thought the views were good to this point in the Blue Ridge, the view at four thousand feet was quite impressive.

Descending The Priest was another task all together. I traveled from over four thousand feet to under one thousand feet in four miles. My hiking speed was amped down through the switchbacks and in the folds of the mountain ridge. I came to a sign for Cripple Creek and of course the song by The Band was running continuously through my head. My knees were tested down this incredible trail.

I was sitting in a grassy area waiting for Sarah for only twenty minutes. She pulled up and we greeted each other with pleasantries. I could not wait to get cleaned up because I felt a little bad I was fairly ripe. Suggesting she roll down the windows was of no use. My stench was real and present. I thanked her for her hospitality and she said it was no problem. Her husband Kevin was cooking us up some steaks for dinner.

After I got cleaned up and less funky, I made myself comfortable in their beautiful home and asked if I could do anything to help for dinner or anything else. They declined and said to relax. I was very excited to be able to clean my sleeping bag. It was the first time it got washed in 831 miles. As my clothes and bag were being washed, I realized I forgot to put in my bandana. I asked Sarah if I could throw it in. When she opened the washer door, she saw the water that was cleaning my things. It was a murky brown hue. I felt horrible, and she laughed it off. She still thought it was disgusting, but she was a good sport about my mustiness.

Dinner was fantastic, and sleep came with ease as I knew I was safe. And I felt loved from their caring for me on this journey. My friend, Greg, had mailed me a new tent to Kevin and Sarah's that was going to keep me dry and warmer than my circus pup tent.

I will forever be in everyone who helped me along this journey's debt for doing so many acts of kindness to me. After dinner, they treated me to some beverages at a local watering hole. For me, it was ginger and Maker's Mark Whisky. For them, it was the stuff of magic in the hops and barley concoction. Beer. Yummy beer. It would come; Maine would have to come.

Instead of hiking the next day up another just about three thousand feet over the Three Ridges Mountain, I worked it out with Sarah and Kevin where I could take a zero day. Sarah dropped me off at a spot with Wi-Fi and some good eats while she and Kevin went to work. I caught up on my *Hiking to Beer* blog and made some necessary phone calls.

Kevin took a half-day, and he and I went back to the house. Sarah let me use her sleeping bag rated for cooler temperatures. I left my sleeping bag behind, and she and Kevin offered to send it to me when I got farther north, where I would needed it. Very sweet of them to do that for me.

The next morning, Sarah and I went to breakfast before she dropped me back off at the suspension bridge. I said good-bye refreshed and ready to tackle Three Ridges Mountain. I destroyed that mountain and continued sight of beautiful views.

When I reached Maupin Field Shelter and had nine miles done before midafternoon, I saw several hikers hiking in from the blue blazed Mau-Har Trail that circles Three Ridges instead of summiting. They looked haggard and exhausted. One of the hikers asked me, "How was the hike over the mountain?"

"Not bad, great views, forgiving trail," I responded

"Oh man, that blue blaze was ridiculous. The trail was rocky and crossed over some rugged terrain." He spoke in shortened breath. A blue blaze trail is a side trail that some hikers use to skip a part of the Appalachian Trail.

A few more hikers came in from the same trail in the same fashion, and he explained to them what I had told them. All the hikers who took the blue blaze regretted not staying on the Appalachian Trail. I didn't take that route, not sure if I would have had the same issues. Watching their exhaustive state, I am happy with the decision to continue my purist way. Only north and cutting the shelter Ys.

I said good-bye to my fellow hiker friends, as I was feeling good to make up some more miles. The next nine miles was mainly ridge walking along a nice, graded trail over some stellar overlooks, Humpback Mountain, and a quarter mile off-trail to a view at The Rocks where I decided to make camp. I could have done it into Paul C. Wolfe Shelter, but I was looking forward to seeing the sunset.

The first time setting up my new tent Greg had gotten me didn't take me long, and when I got into the two-person A-frame castle, it felt comfortable. I sat inside the tent with my feet outside, looking out over the valley, eating my dinner, and enjoying my life at the moment.

I spoke to my friend, Larry, and he agreed to meet me in Waynesboro, Virginia. We agreed on a meet-up spot, and I settled in for the night in my Blue Ridge Mountain home.

The next morning I was a bit groggy; it had rained the evening before, and I stayed warm and dry (the first for me on this trip since hiking 850 miles to this point). I packed up haphazardly, donned pack, and began to increase at a decent pace.

As I came down the switchbacks into Paul C. Wolfe Shelter, I looked down to my left, and I noticed a movement. I got closer, and I saw the movement was a baby fawn. I was within ten feet, and the fawn did not move. It just looked up at me. I stopped for several minutes and talked with the little fella. I think it was something along the lines of how delicious he or she would be when they got older. I said farewell to my new friend and went to the shelter. I took a quick stop to look at the sweet waterfall at Mill Creek just thirty yards from the refuge and then I hiked on.

I walked up to the Paul C. Wolfe Shelter and met Lucky One and Alaska relaxing in the comfort of the nice-sized deck just off the sleeping area of the shelter. I grabbed my food bag out for a snack and looked for my cell phone.

"Oh shit," I said.

"What's wrong?" Lucky One asked.

"I can't find my cell phone."

"It's probably in your pack somewhere."

I started tearing my bag apart and looked through everything. My phone was not there. Remembering all that was on the phone, I panicked because I had hundreds of pictures on it and so many other important things in it. I tried to eat and not think about it for a few minutes.

"Did you stop at all from where you camped?" Lucky One asked.

"I did grab it out to take a picture. I may have dropped it. I think I am going to go back and try to find it. At the least I am going to leave a note in the journal for anyone who may find it."

"Good idea. But you should look in your pack some more."

"Look at my hiker bomb. I am pretty sure I looked everywhere."

And just then I realized I had not checked my hip belt pockets. I grabbed my pack quickly and began digging and then I felt it.

"Oh man! Yes! Yes! Oh man! I was literally having a panic attack over that damn thing."

Lucky One and Alaska had a good laugh at my expense, and I laughed with them. How clumsy of me. I was more than happy I found it. The contents of my backpack were spread out all over the shelter. This time, I made a point of getting a bit more organized as I packed everything back in.

I left my two hiker pals and wished them well on their adventure. They did the same, and I continued into Waynesboro, Virginia. Larry was meeting me in the evening, and I had plenty of time to kill in town.

Chapter NINE

Interstate 64 was abuzz as I climbed over the railing onto the highway. It took less than fifteen minutes to get a ride to the YMCA in Waynesboro, where they offered free showers and a beautiful place to camp. The folks at the YMCA were very friendly and explained to me where the camping area was in town. I left after getting cleaned up and went in search of a camping spot.

The South River runs peacefully through town. When I crossed the bridge at South Wayne Avenue, I looked down to my right and saw a sweet little grassy area. I walked down to the base of the bridge under the shade of a peeling birch tree and set up my tent. I climbed in and got my area ready to sleep for the night because although I was going out with Larry, I was planning for the next morning and getting on the trail right away.

Once I got my tent situated the way I wanted, I zipped it up and walked around town. Waynesboro is a friendly hiker and adventurer town. The local town folk are very friendly and encouraging. I got a lot of compliments on my beard and several words of support of my continued hike north.

Larry and I met up at an all-you-can-eat Chinese buffet. I showed him his beat-up ukulele, White Blaze, aptly named. He was impressed at her sound, even after the bumps and bruises she had endured the last 860 miles. Without a case or any protective cover, she was in pretty good shape.

Larry treated dinner and asked if I wanted to have a drink. I still wanted to hang out, so he and I went to two local breweries in the area. The first brewery was the same one Kevin and Sarah had taken me. I again ordered a Makers Mark and ginger. Larry got something hoppy. We saw Sarah and Kevin out at the bar and they were apparently confused. I introduced them to my friend, Larry, and they asked some obvious questions.

"No, I hiked into Waynesboro. . . . Yes, I am still hiking."

We said our good-byes as we headed to the next brewery. Larry snapped a pretty cool shot of me in front of that beer factory, then we saddled up to the bar for a drink.

"I'll take a Maker's Mark and ginger."

"Sorry, just beer and wine."

"Just beer and wine?"

"Yep, sorry."

"I'll take a Merlot."

Larry ordered another hoppy goodness, and we sat there checking out the scene. There were a lot of people enjoying the outdoor sitting area that looked out to a magical silhouette of the mountains I just finished climbing the last few days. It was immaculate outside, and the stars were cramming for attention. I missed the taste of beer looking up at that sky. What a goal, giving up beer. I think that motivation in itself kept me very focused.

Larry and I finished for the evening, and he still needed to drive back to the Hinkle Ukulele shop and his Stafford, Virginia, home. I thanked him for coming all the way to see me and for the trail music in White Blaze. He dropped me off at the restaurant where we ate earlier, and I began to walk back to my camp.

Miss Janet, the ultimate trail angel, was in the area, and I wanted to see her. She tried to describe where they were over the phone, but unfortunately, I wasn't able to find her. I felt sad, but I also needed to sleep and get up early to get out on the trail.

While lying in my tent that night, I thought about my childhood. My mom, stepdad, two sisters, and I lived in a nice home on Fourth Street in Emporium, Pennsylvania. At around two a.m. on April 1, 1990, when I was sitting around the house doing nothing, I got bored, so I grabbed my parents' car keys to their cherry red Ford Thunderbird and headed out the door. At the age of twelve, I got behind the wheel and drove down the street. It was around one in the morning, and I went for a joy ride around the town. I was driving back and forth on Fourth Street, and I began feeling sleepy. I dozed off for just a second and then . . .

Crash!

Immediately I was woken and uninjured. I did have my seat belt on and quickly put the car in reverse and drove up the hillside, called Sixth Street Extension, a street I was familiar with from living at the top of the hill until I was eight years old. When I parked the car in a driveway at the top of the street where it makes a large curve and drops into Plank Hallow, I assessed the damage to the front of the cherry red Ford Thunderbird; it was not good. I had panicked a bit before I derived a plan to cover up my story.

Sleep came in my reverie by the river, and I woke up to the sounds of traffic heading over the bridge. I rubbed the "sleepies" out of my eyes and started packing up. I shook my head to juggle my thoughts a bit to face the day. I knew I had to quickly get out of camp to catch a ride from an angel headed to work.

My pack was a bit heavy from my resupply, but I needed to stop at the outfitters heading out of town. So I just walked the mile to the store. I grabbed a buff (bandanna) and another guide because I had left mine in the shuttle back at the James River Bridge. I needed the information from the handbook for mileage checks, but, more importantly, locations of my hydration. Even though I was hiking to beer, technically I was walking to water at every chance. To become dehydrated is to become an unfortunate victim of the wilderness. With the guide weighing just a bit over a pound, I grimaced at even more weight on my back. Put up or shut up, as the saying goes.

As soon as I left the outfitter, I saw Miss Janet and her big white Appalachian Trail shuttle coming up the road. I waved her down. We gave hugs and I thanked her for picking me up. The sun was shining with a few straggling clouds here and there when Miss Janet dropped me off. I threw her a few bucks for gas and gave her another big hug before walking back to where I got off the trail.

This next section was the beginning of the Shenandoah National Park, or the "Shennies" as many call the big park. A short road walk before a hike into the wooded ridgeline brought hikers to the registration box. Any overnight hiker needs the paper attached to their pack so park officials can see where the hikers are from. It also informs authorities where the hiker got on the trail and where they intend to get off. There was a place for dates, too, but I left that blank because I didn't know how long it was going to take to hike a hundred miles of park.

I met up with Oak, a fellow thru-hiker from New Jersey. I enjoyed his company and we hiked well together. My pace in the Shennies was much better, and I was tackling the mountainsides well. Bears Den Mountain was the first mountain we came to. It was a unique mountain equipped with tractor seats that were affixed firmly in the ground for hikers to take a break. I sat and waited for Oak and looked up at several gigantic communications towers. Oh, technology, we're all connected by a few microwaves and personal buttons to press. Extraordinary and scary at the same time.

The next few days Oak and I crossed over the Blue Ridge Parkway several times. And these little park restaurants, called "waysides," served up some of the best blackberry milkshakes I have ever tasted. We had several naps at these grassy wayside areas and humped it up and over mountains, into gaps, across ridgelines, and to the best water source I had tasted since being on the trail.

Black Rock Hut was located a quarter mile off-trail, and the water source was to the front and right of the hut. I could hear the rushing water, and when I saw the steel pipe protruding out of the side of the hillside, I was in awe. In the back of my mind I thought I should probably filter, but being so close to the top of Trayfoot Mountain, I opted to "raw dog" it (or not filter). I filled my cup and took the water right to the head. Euphoric is the feeling I felt when drinking that water. Ahhh, the little things.

After camping at Back Rock Hut, I woke the next morning with a pep in my step. Six miles into my hike for the day after summiting Trayfoot Mountain and across the ridges leading to Loft Mountain Campground, I turned a sharp corner. I saw it—his ass was so fat, right there, less than thirty feet in front of me on the trail. My first black bear encounter was with his big butt wobbling in front of me. I did not slow down, but I sped up a bit.

"Hey!" I yelled.

The bear did not talk back, but he did look over his shoulder at me and made a "fffumfffffooo."

The huge black bear was disappointed I inconvenienced his day. A few snaps of my hiking poles above my head and the beast took a sharp left-hand turn up into the mountain laurel. I passed within five feet of him as he doubled his step up into the woods.

"Get outta here, bear!" I yelled at him. "Ain't nobody got no time for that!" I said as I laughed, heading up the trail.

The Loft Mountain Campground was busy with campers. I stopped and talked to a few people before using the real bathroom. The water there tasted funny, but I contributed it to campground well water. Oh well, I was hydrated.

During the night I heard some animal just outside of the Pinefield Hut. When I illuminated my headlamp outside near the fire pit, I saw a bobcat eating on something. I yelled at him, too, but he did not care for my voice and I heard him hiss. At that point I decided to let him or her eat and went back to sleep.

A few hikers had slept in the same hut and I asked them if they heard me yelling at the bobcat. They said they had not, and I don't think they believed that it happened.

Near the fire pit, I saw a bag of figs that were ripped open. I assumed that is what my bobcat friend was nibbling on—although it must not have liked it that much because there were a lot left. I also thought my yell may have scared it enough to move on.

My friend, Adrienne, and her husband, Chris, said they would let me come and get cleaned up and get some rest at their house not far from the trail. I grew up closely with Adi and her family and was very appreciative of them taking me in. I called her as I hiked from Pinefield Hut. She let me know that Chris would pick me up at Lewis Mountain Campground that evening. I was about eight miles away after I hung up with her. I steadied my pace and arrived at the campground pretty worn out from some big ascents and knee-biting descents.

Chris arrived and I threw my pack in his car. I was pretty ripe smelling, but it didn't seem to bother him too much. I told him about the trail life and the magic that was prevalent out on the journey. We got to their house and I enjoyed a hot shower and getting into some clean clothes. They all got me some trail snacks and they made some amazing homemade meals while I rested and energized. I would be sad to leave them to get back on the trail after taking my last zero day (unbeknownst to me) until New Jersey. Adi and her son, Jaxson, took me back to the trail. I gave hugs and said good-bye as I grabbed and donned pack for the about thousandth time on this journey.

Virginia hosts the longest stretch through any of the other fourteen Appalachian Trail states at almost 550 miles. The exultation hikers feel leaving one state setting and entering another is an enormous feeling of accomplishment. Because Virginia takes so long to hike through from the borer of Tennessee into West Virginia, some hikers get what is called the "Virginia Blues." While hiking from Lewis Mountain Campground and into an area I was very familiar with, these "Virginia Blues" did not bother me like they bothered others.

I was traveling just south of Big Meadows Campground at a very quick pace. Ahead of me, I could see a group of some sort gathered on the trail. They saw me as I approached and made way. I did not slow down as I passed the group and a Park Ranger who was giving a tour. Less than ten yards away, I heard behind me . . . "Hey! Do you want a Snickers?" the park ranger had called out.

I turned on my heal and still did not slow down. I saw that he was holding it up in front of him. I approached him, politely grabbed the candy bar, and turned again on my heal. I did not lose ground as I humped a bit faster up the slightly graded ascent of the trail. Over my shoulder as I continued north I yelled, "Thanks!" and disappeared around the next bend.

Later Oak came into Rock Spring Hut where I was getting some water.

"Did you see the group back there?" he asked.

"Yep," I replied.

"Did you get a Snickers?"

"Uh-huh."

"Didn't they stop you and ask you a bunch of questions?"

I began laughing hysterically as he grinned at me.

"They didn't, did they?" he asked.

"No, no they didn't. The ranger learned from his mistake. I guess we are like talking bears out here in the wilderness."

I told Oak how I got out of the question and answer session. Not that I wouldn't have. Had he held back the Snickers and explained I needed to answer a few questions, maybe I would have complied. But, he didn't. So I continued my way. Oak and I continue to have a good laugh, and I exclaimed, "Ain't nobody got no time for that!"

I hiked on just before Skyland Resort and Restaurant because of a buffet that was given two thumbs up by other hiker friends. I made camp around Hawskbill Gap, woke up the next morning and hiked on. When I came to the Skyland Stables, I stopped and watched the horses and mules roam around until the flies began to find me good company. Those little bastards.

"Would you like the buffet, sir?" For a grimy looking hiker guy, they were very polite there.

"Yes, please, I will have the buffet."

It was Father's Day 2013 and the restaurant overlooked the Blue Ridge Mountains and the valley below. The farms in the distance looked like little grassy patches. Inside, the tables were all cloth covered and windows that spread across the open area. The hostess sat me away from the better-smelling guests. I left my bag and headed straight for the restroom to wash my hands. During the walk back to my table, I looked down at all the buffet had to offer and I grabbed a plate. It had cantaloupe, grapes, water-melon, strawberries, blackberries, raspberries, and two flavors of yogurt, sausage, bacon, Canadian bacon, biscuits, gravy, and a partridge in a pear tree.

While reflecting on my life, I was very thankful. Even though it was Father's Day and I hadn't yet called either my step-dad or my biological father, I was thinking of them. A loner in a lonely world can only do the amount he is set out to do on this blue ball that spins in its simple problems. My appreciation runs deep for those who have helped me throughout my life. I may not have it all, but I have all I need.

When I finished up, I began my trek north yet again. Several day hikers were out in the area of Stony Man Summit. At 4,011 feet, Stony Man Mountain has an incredible trail leading up to the highest elevation in the Shennies along the AT. The weather con-tinued to be pleasant as I hiked on for the next two days.

I was looking forward to seeing my cousins, Jennifer, Robby, and Lucas, as they were meeting me in Front Royal, Virginia, to shower me yet again with their continued love and support. Most important to them though, soap and water. I called them while I was hanging out at Elk Wallow Wayside. I also talked to my friend, Ryan, who was trying to plan a hike with me somewhere in Pennsylvania. My thoughts were racing as I was get-ting closer to mile one thousand of the Appalachian Trail. It all just seemed so surreal.

_____That cherry red Thunderbird, in my twelve year old body I assessed the damage, I was in shock. I got back into the damaged car and drove it back home. I parked it in the same spot on the road next to the Episcopal Church. Quietly, I returned to my room and went to sleep.

The next morning I was shaken awake by my mom, who was frantic. She told me someone had run into the Thunderbird and that the police were on their way. I feigned ignorance, but not the shock. The police did not speak to me at the beginning of the investigation because they believed I had been sleeping throughout the night. I did feel bad, but I also didn't want to go to jail.

Two months passed and my grades in school were the best they had ever been. I didn't miss a homework assignment, and my test scores were good. Although I enjoyed school at times, I did not apply my full potential, and I believe it was for several reasons. One, I looked at the whole school experience as a cockfight. The social order of things was dictated by many levels of who you were and who your parents were. At one point during those two months, I attended my uncle's navy retirement. Uncle Tim saw right through me and said outright, "Lloyd wrecked that car." It was painful to hear my mom defend me so much, but I still wasn't budging on letting anyone know about my secret.

_____

It was in Mr. McGraw's class when I heard over the speaker system, "Mr. McGraw?"

"Yes?" he called back.

"Could you please send Lloyd Fink up to the office please?"

"Yes."

I had been in a deep sleep on my desk; slobber drooled down from my lips to my desktop below. A nice little slobber puddle formed. I woke up and wiped my mouth just as the speaker made the initial scratching sound. I listened to the exchange while a multitude of questions ran through my head. I was doing pretty well in school, mainly thanks to some friends by my locker who had their assignments completed. A quick copy and paste and I was ready to go. There were no indications of why I was being called to the office.

Mr. McGraw nodded in my direction and I moved slowly to the door. I heard over my shoulder some chiding from my classmates, but I continued to walk to the office. The hall was quiet. I did not see anyone until I turned the corner. I looked up to see my step-dad standing at the secretaries' window.

He walked toward me without saying a word. I just followed behind him. I asked him where we were going. No response. He just drove through town along Fourth Street to the other side of the little village, across the railroad tracks, past the ball fields, and then we pulled in the parking lot of the Pennsylvania State Police building.

"They are going to ask you some questions about the car. Answer truthfully."

"Okay."

When I walked into the office, I saw my sisters, my uncles, and a few town riffraff. I was the only riffraff there at this point, though. An officer asked me to take a seat and said someone would be with me shortly. I got some information from my sister about a lie detector test everyone was taking.

My hands began to clam up; my heart rate started to elevate; nervous anxiety engulfed my whole spirit.

"Lloyd."

"Yeah?"

"Go on back."

"Okay."

The black box with wires protruding out in the small area of the room got me jumping out of my skin. The man running the machine began droning on in explaining how everything worked. I had to sign a paper and agreed to tell the truth. He hooked me up with a finger clamp, and then he wrapped some cords around my chest. The questions began, and sweat started to show on my brow.

Once he was finished and took all the wires off of me, I showed a pale white.

"Do you have something to tell me?"

"Yes."

"You took the car that night, didn't you?"

"Yes."

"And you wrecked it?"

"Yes."

"I'm going to bring your dad in now and you're going to tell him."

"Okay."

He walked out of the office and then both he and my step-dad walked in. Both men stared down at me, and I knew my step-dad knew. I didn't need to say the words.

"Tell your dad what you told me."

"I wrecked the car."

"Okay." My step-dad said.

"He is free to go home with you. We'll be in touch."

"All right." My step-dad responded.

They shook hands and we left the building. Telling my mom was a disaster. To say she was upset was a complete and utter understatement. They sent me to my room. Although I felt guilty, I also felt relief that the lies were no longer weighing on me. I received a probation officer and was sent to three different facilities over the next eight months: A mental hospital, a detention center, and a halfway house. One thing was sure: I realized I did not want to be in these kinds of facilities as an adult.

Chapter TEN

With a pretty uneventful hike out of the Shennies and into Front Royal, Virginia, I was excited to see my cousins. I was able to get a ride to the post office where my awesome ma sent me a trail magic package and some great words of encouragement. After leaving the post office, I immediately got a ride from a lovely lady to the hotel where I was meeting up with Robby, Jennifer, and Lucas. I arrived first and took a nap on the bench outside while waiting for them. Robby honked as he pulled up. They got out, and we all gave each other big hugs. I hadn't seen them for several months, and it was good to catch up.

We went up to the room, and I did the routine of getting hiker trash musk off my body. My feet were stinking up to high heaven, so I hid my nasty boots outside in a bush. We all laughed and carried on as we all like to do about silly stuff cousins do.

The four of us went out to eat and ate some delicious surf and turf. I put down about eight glasses of water filled with about eight lemon wedges. The waitress saw I had some food in my beard and I asked, "Would you mind getting in for me?" Then I stuck out my chin.

She looked down at me and gave me a sideways look. "No." And then she walked away.

Belly laughs ensued and we made our way back to the hotel room.

A solid night's sleep in a very comfortable hotel bed and I was ready to hike on. I organized my pack again, and we all jumped into the truck. At the trailhead, we took a bunch of pictures and cheered on some Cheer Wine. I asked Lucas if he wanted to hike a bit with me, but he wasn't feeling it. I gave them all hugs and began down the trail, dancing and skipping along the way.

The three hundred-foot climb and marble-sized raindrops began landing on my head in a torrent. I grabbed my raincoat quickly but had already gotten soaked before I could get it on. Jim and Molly Denton Shelter was only five miles from the road where I just left my cousin. I did not want to end my hike there, but the shelter was more like a house, a well-manicured lawn with a pavilion at the front.

I watched the rain slam down on the open yard as I began drying off beneath the roof of the shelter. The terrain was rough and tumbling the next few days. There were some adult hiker issues in the presence of a large Boy Scout troop. Two grown men were yelling and cursing at each other because one of them snored too loudly in the shelter.

It was high drama, and I told them both to "shut the hell up."

Once I continued up and down several small one to three hundred-foot hills, I ran into Polly. Polly, her hiking friend, Momma, and I met in the Smokies; we also hung out lying in the grass in Damascus. I was set up at Sam Moore Shelter when she invited me to come along with her to her mom's house.

"Of course. Can you wait a few minutes while I pack up?"

"Yeah, but hurry. Momma is meeting us at Bears Den Hostel."

Momma was Polly's hiking partner in the Smokies when I met them, and they both were an inspiration. Great hikers and positive, uplifting people. I am so happy to know them.

Darkness set as we made our way into Bears Den Rocks. Momma was in the parking lot waiting for us. I made a point to poke my head into the hostel to see if there was anyone I knew there, but not too many hikers were out in the joint areas. The hostels have pretty strict rules and for good reason. Keeping people safe is a constant challenge when running such a business.

Polly's mom was so helpful and accommodating to complete strangers. Momma made some homemade goodness, and we all just enjoyed the conversation for a few hours before heading off to bed.

We all made our way to town to get some coffee the next morning. Starbucks was the consensus, but when we pulled in, I saw across the parking lot the best coffee joint in America: Dunkin' Donuts, or as Uncle Tim calls it, "Dunts." Polly and Momma walked into Starbucks, and I walked toward Dunts. "I'll be right there," I said over my shoulder.

"One black amazingly delicious large coffee to go, please."

"Comin' right up!"

I walked into Starbucks in all my rebellion and sat down with Polly and Momma. They laughed at me as I took a picture of the Starbucks logo on the window with my Dunts coffee in front of it. We were all smiles as we sat, enjoying the moment. Polly was getting concerned for me because it was getting close to midafternoon and I needed to get back on the trail.

"No hurry. Whenever you're ready," I said.

"No. I know how it feels. I will get you back," Polly responded.

It was so thoughtful of her to take me back and remind me that I was going to be hitting a milestone of ONE THOUSAND MILES HIKED. I put that in caps because the accomplishment was more than huge. She dropped me at the very busy intersection of VA 7 and 679. I thanked her and told her to thank her mom for me, as well.

It was not a far hike until I hit the sign that read "one thousand AT miles." I was by myself, so I put my phone on a ten second timer and set it on my backpack opposite the sign. There was a lot of trial and error with getting a good shot, but eventually, I got an acceptable one and hiked on.

The Blackburn Appalachian Trail Center is a bit off the trail, and although I only walked seven miles, the area around the center was welcoming, so I set my tent up near the main building and hung out with some other hikers on the porch. The Blackburn Center caretakers gave me a soda and a brownie before I headed over to my tent to catch up on some journaling.

Up and at 'em the next morning to make a casual hike into Harpers Ferry and the head-quarters of the Appalachian Trail Conservancy. My emotions were running pretty deep as I hiked another milestone. Out of Virginia and into West "by God" Virginia.

I remember taking a field trip to Harpers Ferry. A unique town, three states border its community: Virginia, West Virginia, and Maryland. We learned about John Brown and his rebel abolitionists. The field trip took place a few weeks before Christmas, as I recall. Our chaperones allowed us to walk around without "thumb on head" supervision. As I walked around the small hillside town, I had many flashbacks as I watched several tourists walking on the AT, just for the fun of it. I was snapped to when I saw out the corner of my eye a familiar white and blue van belonging to one of the coolest trail angels on the Appalachian Trail.

Miss Janet was driving across the Shenandoah Bridge with several hikers in her van. She beeped, and I gave a wide smile and waved vigorously. On top of her van were several inner tubes. Somewhere hikers were going on a river adventure. I was happy to see them, but in a way, I wanted to be tubing down a river somewhere.

Tourists hiking around the paths of Harpers Ferry were watching me as I walked beside a familiar Jefferson Rock and into town. I stopped at the PO for a package, but unfortunately, not all the things I needed were there. My mom had sent me a new pair of boots that were not there. She called the post office and called me back to tell me they did not have them, but she was going to send Uncle Tim and Aunt Gin a message to pick me some up. I was going to see them the next day and it would work out.

My boots were tattered and falling apart. I used some glue to hold them together for the next twenty-four hours before meeting up with my aunt and uncle.

I grabbed a large pizza before visiting the ATC. The good people working and volunteering there are some great souls. I used their hiker facilities and then got my thru-hiker photo out front. In the picture are White Blaze, one of my slices, and my smiling mug. I thanked them and began my hike back to the trail.

The AT crosses Byron Memorial Footbridge across the Potomac River and into my sixth state, Maryland, USA. The bridge is also a railroad bridge. The water below was quiet, but it was still rushing pretty good along toward Washington, DC. The C & O Canal Towpath greeted me as I stepped down from the bridge. I was so in my little world that I didn't pay any attention as the walking confused me. I zigged when I should have zagged.

About a mile and a half later, I realized my error and turned around. With a double time in my step, I passed some hikers heading into Harpers Ferry from their campsite to resupply. We smiled and gave each other pleasantries.

The trail continued on the C & O Canal Towpath for almost three miles before cutting up the mountain and Weverton Cliffs. I was practically running and jumping up the hillside. I could barely feel any pain or discomfort. I was "gettin' it!"

A little hike into the Ed Garvey Shelter and I set up camp to look forward to some quality time with Uncle Tim and Aunt Ginger. Once I got settled in and a fire going, I researched the water source for the shelter. The guide said that the source was almost a half a mile down a steep trail in front of the shelter.

With my water bag in my hand and almost ready to leave, I heard footsteps coming toward the haven.

"Hi!" came the voice entering the shelter.

"Hey, how are you doing?"

"Not bad. Pretty awesome hiking day."

"Yeah it is! Where are you coming from?"

"Around Dahlgren Backpack Campground. You headed north? I highly recommend it."

"My trail friend, Lil Bear, told me about that site, but I am hanging with some relatives tomorrow. I will probably end up passing it up, unfortunately."

"Are you headed for water?"

"Well I was. You want to make a deal?"

"Maybe, depends on the deal."

"I have four slices of pizza from Harpers Ferry here, and, well, the water is way down the hill. If you fill up my water, I'll give you two slices."

Before I even finished that sentence, my new trail friend, Mike, took my container bag and was headed down the hillside.

"Be right back." He laughed as he practically jogged away.

While he was getting water, I spread some coals of the fire to one side and placed the cardboard from the pizza box with the four slices on top of a few rocks to melt the cheese. Ingenious idea is what it was.

About thirty minutes later and some hot pies, Mike was back with water. He and I sat by the fire enjoying our za.

"Thanks, man."

"No," I said, "thank you."

Mike was still sleeping when I ventured out in a light sprinkle from above and a rocky terrain underfoot into Gathland State Park. As I waited for Uncle Tim and Aunt Ginger, a hiker, by the name of Glacier Freeze, his sister, and brother were attempting the four-state challenge. The four-state challenge is hiking from Virginia through West Virginia, Maryland, and into Pennsylvania in twenty-four hours. Several of my hiking friends accomplished this in 2013. Glacier Freeze was very fast, and I knew he was going to get the almost sixty miles done. Had I not been meeting my aunt and uncle, I would have never attempted that.

The pavilion at Gatham State Park has a huge seating area with a deep barbecue pit. As I was sitting there, I thought about the foodstuffs I could conjure up that would make Ron Swanson proud to consume.

Glacier Freeze and his siblings just started up the hill and through the open field when Aunt Ginger and Uncle Tim arrived to pick me up. I yelled my good luck out to them, and they waved good-bye.

Uncle Tim and Aunt Ginger spoiled me with surf and turf. Then we went over to the Charles Town casino where I bet on horse number nine to win. I snapped a picture with my ticket and popcorn as the jockey for horse number nine ran first across the finish line. We went to the hotel, where I had a restful night's sleep.

Back at Gatham State Park, we exchanged hugs, and I was back out on the AT dirt. I passed on the quarter-mile hike into Crampton Gap Shelter, instead heading on toward Washington Monument State Park and picnic area. I did make a pit stop off at Dahlgren Backpack Campground to use their flushable toilets. Less than a mile and I received some trail magic from Glacier Freeze's dad of some fresh fruits and a Gatorade . . . yep, Glacier Freeze. I thanked him and headed up to the first president's monument.

Some guys were up at the base of the monument dressed in Civil War-era Union soldier uniforms. They were doing a reenactment as a part of the signal corps. There was a set of flags they used to communicate Confederate soldiers' movements. I asked if they would mind if I got my picture with them. They didn't, and Yukon agreed to snap a few before he and I climbed the steps to observe the view of the Maryland lowlands. It was an awe-inspiring view, and the reenactors made me think about how life would have been like during that period. Before cars, phones, and so many other incredible advancements in our human history, we made it.

I did not stay long, as I wanted to make it to Pine Knob Shelter for the night. Yukon said he was going to stay back, and I wished him well as I donned pack and headed out.

The hike from the monument to Pine Knob Shelter and across Interstate 70 was pretty smooth. The shelter was a tenth of a mile off of the AT, and instead of staying there, I opted to hike less than two more miles to a vista and campground, called Annapolis Rocks.

Annapolis Rocks had a caretaker, and I asked her if there were tent sites available. She said that there were and to head down the trail and pick any open site. I thanked her and walked toward the edge of the mountain.

I found a lovely spot, grabbed some water, made some dinner, and explored the area. The rocks jettisoned out in several areas. Great seating and a wonderful set of views across the mountain's ridgeline. For over forty-five minutes, I sat and reflected on the last approximately 1,100 miles. Then I headed back to my camp spot for some sleep before heading out the next morning. Sleep took me like a thief in the night.

Chapter ELEVEN

I bid good-bye to the caretaker of Annapolis Rocks after packing up and hiking to the front of the campground. The sun was shining as I continued for the next seventeen miles of Maryland and made my way home, well, to my home state of Pennsylvania. Home, I was taught, is where the heart is. And we can never get away from our hearts.

I had seen Mamachip at several road crossings, and she was kind enough to give me some trail magic of soda and snacks each and every time. She did this for several hikers, some more handy than others. Nonetheless appreciated by most hikers for sure.

My straps to my backpack were fraying, and I had called the company to get a new pack, but they only offered to replace the front shoulder strap. I was expecting the package to arrive at the South Mountain, Pennsylvania, post office. I was looking forward to replacing the shoulder belts. I had been unable to adjust for comfort during many miles.

Yukon and I stayed at Ensign Cowall Shelter about eighteen miles from the Pennsylvania–Maryland state line with a few other hikers who were about. He and I both woke up and began packing up, but he decided to not hike out with me. We wished each other luck as I hoofed it hard to state number seven on my Appalachian Trail thru-hike.

Surprisingly, I had a really good pace when I got to Pen Mar County Park. The Mason–Dixon line was only a few hundred feet down the trail. When I entered the park, I noticed a pop machine. My mouth was watering for a pop for last sixteen miles of hiking. I saw a park employee in an ATV, known as a Gator, pull up to me as I approached the pop machine.

"Brawken," he said in a slur.

"What?"

"Yep, kids busted it up to get some pop out."

"Aw, no way, man."

"Sorry," he said as he drove away.

Just as I started feeling sorry for myself, I saw a vehicle approach and a big bearded guy get out. It was Yukon. Instead of hiking from the Ensign Shelter, Yukon decided to get a ride. I chided him a bit, but that was fun to see him. Hike your hike, damn it!

The park didn't allow camping, but they were less strict with thru-hikers, so Yukon and I stealth camped in the pavilion. He took one side of the stage and I took the other. Once I got my area set up, I walked over to an overlook that had seating. The sun was setting and it was a glorious watching of the shades of oranges, blues, and pinks casting across the Maryland skyline looking into the great state of Pennsylvania.

I woke up the next morning and Yukon was moving hesitantly.

"Are you hiking out with me today, or are you gonna get a ride to Maine?" I laughed and chided.

"I am gonna hike out." He chuckled and smiled at my assholery.

There was a well-liked sign that used to be next to the Maryland/Pennsylvania border, but it was not there when I arrived. I was disappointed a bit. The cherry color rectangular sign simply read, The Mason Dixon Line.

We approached Buena Vista Road, and I noticed behind me that he was lagging and pausing at the road.

"I think I am gonna go into Waynesboro," he called.

"Ah, man, I was hoping for a hiking partner today."

"Sorry, I'll catch up."

"All right, man, see you in Maine!"

"Be safe. See you later."

A few miles up the trail, I ran into Chipmunk hiking strong through the Pennsylvania Wilds. She was singing loudly, and I think I heard her call out, "Get outta here, bear." Ha. Maybe.

"Hey!"

"Hi, Uke."

"How are you? How is your ma?"

"Good. She is doing good. I am meeting her at South Mountain this afternoon."

"Oh cool. If you talk to her before you get there, can you ask her if I can get a ride to the post office to pick up my shoulder straps for my pack?"

"Sure," she said.

Chipmunk and I hiked into Deer Lick Shelters for a quick break. A few hikers were still hanging out there, and one of them stated that the Mason–Dixon sign was around somewhere. I was asking where it was, and he pointed to one of the two shelters. I walked over and found two halves of the sign lying just outside of the three-sided structure.

Chipmunk and I took our pictures with it and sent a few to her ma over the interwebs. I suggested we take the sign with us and give it to a park ranger if we saw one. The other hiker said he had already decided to do that, so Chipmunk and I hiked on to South Mountain, where Mama Chip was going to be meeting her.

It was good seeing Mama Chip, and she was so kind in driving me to the post office. The only problem was the backpack company sent the wrong straps, and now I was at the point of tying and sewing it. What a pain in the ass. I immediately called them and explained what I needed. After the customer service representative had heard me out, he agreed to send me a replacement backpack as long as I sent the destroyed pack back to them. I quickly accepted and gave him the information he needed for me to pick it up in Delaware Water Gap at the outfitter there. Mama Chip took us back to the trail, where we met up with none other than Jo Cool and her partner, B-Man.

I had not seen Jo Cool since our night hike out of Troutville, Virginia. Her awesome partner, B-Man, Chipmunk, and I all dragged into Caledonia State Park together. The hiking was nice with the great company that kept up a good pace. We all were looking forward to jumping in the "poo." And, of course, hoped for some of that sweet trail magic.

Mama chip met us on the trail at the highway just before the park and drove us all in her Chip-mobile. The truck camper was roomy and comfortable as we sat in the back as she turned us into a magnificent sunny day at the most beautiful Caledonia State Park.

All of us jumped out and hiked over to the "poo" entrance. Several hikers were all relaxing just outside and we all talked about trail stuff. I decided to hike over to the road and hike back so I didn't have to when I returned to the trail. Being the crazy purist as I was, I put on my pack and told my friends I would return momentarily.

About three minutes into hiking, I saw Gilgamesh and his monster rebar hiking poles. His arms were becoming behemoth style. He looked at me and commented that I was going the wrong way. I told him I would be right back. I tapped the spot where I just got off the trail and giggled to myself why I didn't just hike over instead of getting a ride.

Probably because I just want to experience everything, in each and every moment. It's a thing; we all should strive to live in the moment. Less stuff, more experiences makes Jack a better man. Right, Jack?

Back at the pool, I set my pack by some hiker folks, changed into my clean shorts, showered my stink off, and then headed to the very cold pool water. Splashing and laughter commenced for a few hours. At around five, I decided to hike on since my body temperature was down and the walk up the next mountain looked to be a bit steep.

It was around five in the evening. Gilgamesh decided to hike on, as well. He was meeting up with a cool trail hiker, by the name of Sly Fox. The heat was getting to us as we climbed the mountain past two charming shelters. Quarry Gap Shelters had a nice setup. I noticed a lovely seating area. There were pots with an assortment of colorful flowers falling over the pots' edges. I stopped, signed the register, and hiked on.

Chapter TWELVE

We hiked into Pine Grove Furnace to the "event." Several things happen as you get close to Pine Grove Furnace State Park, the first being the official halfway point of the Appalachian Trail. At 1,094.5 miles of hiking, there is somewhat of a jolt. I know I felt the emotions of the day and I believe Chipmunk also felt it. We were both sore and ready to end our day. The second is an Appalachian Trail tradition of eating a half-gallon of ice cream in a timed situation. A half-gallon of ice cream at the halfway point of hiking . . . "awesome" is just one word to describe the feelings that flow from the hikers' spirits.

Chipmunk was doing a talk for the young folk of The Goddard School. The talk was on the front porch of the Iron Mansion Hostel. She invited us to listen to her speak about her experiences on the Appalachian Trail. Chipmunk is a great speaker, and she answered the kids' question with clarity and comedy. They were in awe of one of their peers hiking from Georgia to Maine. Myself, Gilgamesh, and Sly Fox, who were also there for her presentation, thought likewise.

We left the school kids to their normal American lives as our abnormal selves made it to the ice cream challenge. I decided on Neapolitan because if I was going to eat a half-gallon of ice cream in less than a minute, I wanted three flavors. A news crew arrived as we were preparing to munch. They were there to interview our celebrity friend. And with celebrity comes perks.

Mama Chip told us that the park ranger extended an invite for all of us to stay at the campground. We accepted graciously. The Chip-mobile carried us to the Pine Grove Furnace campsites. Much needed libations were acquired at a local store. The night was filled with laughter, Maker's Mark with ginger, and of course . . . watermelon.

I hung around my ice cream challenge folks into Boiling Springs. The hike was arduous over rock boulders and through several rock fields. Pennsylvania for thru-hikers is called "Rocksylvania." Many ankles had succumbed to the rigors of trail life through the large state. Once I got out of the mountains just before Boiling Springs, the sky opened up into a cornfield. I hiked to an area used for camping and began setting up, but I realized it was not the spot where I was meeting up with everyone. I packed back up and began heading into town.

Boiling Springs is a neat little town. I set up my camping area and walked into town. The trail passes on the north side of Children's Lake. At the ATC Mid-Atlantic Regional Office, hikers can check in, use some amenities, get trail information, and hike on down the trail.

I picked up a magic trail package at the post office, and I was happy as a pig in shit at the goodies inside from Aunt Gin, Uncle Tim, and Cousins Jennifer, Robby, Lucas, and Robyn. We had a good dinner and went to bed down for the night. My tent was set up directly behind the Chip-mobile, and I woke up the next morning with big miles on my mind. Unfortunately, a pool would curb any aspirations of that.

Mama Chip, Chipmunk, Talker, and I went to breakfast. There was a nice café, and we had an excellent meal. It was dense and delicious.

Gilgamesh and Sly Fox got a room at the Allenberry Resort Inn and Playhouse. The pool at the resort was calling my name, as it was still hot. A big storm was forecast for later in the day. A quick drink at the Allenberry Bar with Gilgamesh, Sly Fox, and Mama Chip was refreshing. Gilgamesh treated me to a nice straight-up whiskey. I told him I had to hike out, but he was clear that he wanted to party a bit more. Although the resort was very welcoming, I made the choice to hike out.

The guide showed the next twelve miles with little to no elevation gain or drop. I was happy about this and bumped my steps up. By myself, I noticed a storm rolling in. "Auntie Em! Auntie Em!" The winds began whipping, and I was running the next several miles. There was a trail angel in the area, according to a note at one of the trail crossings. I called the number, and someone answered right away.

"Hi, I saw your note about a place to stay. I wouldn't be calling, but there is a thunderstorm I would like to get out of."

"Oh, yeah. Are you okay with coming to a party? My boyfriend and I are going to a house party. You are more than welcome to join."

"Sure. That sounds fun."

"We'll be there soon to pick you up."

"Thank you!"

The three of us went to the low-key house party, where we enjoyed some good grub and I drank a few rum and cokes. I was asked many questions, especially when I declined beer.

"So you haven't drank a beer since?"

"Last September?"

"Wow, that is impressive."

"Thanks. I didn't give it up altogether. When I summit Katahdin in Maine, I will drink my first beer after over a year."

"That is some motivation."

"It is *the* motivation."

We laughed about how crazy the idea is of making a goal, giving up something, and getting the reward for that something after the goal is complete. Some would say it is silly, but that one little tick in the back of my brain telling to keep moving was huge. Keep with the steps. One step at a time. It certainly may not be a big deal to some people, but for me it was the deal.

Later that evening we went back to their apartment, where I slept like a baby. Instead of hiking out early as planned, I was meeting up with my friend, Greg, who was a mentor for me in my young juvenile delinquent stages of my childhood. He was also the angel who sent me a leak-proof tent back in Roseland, Virginia.

Kathleen dropped me off at the Clarks Ferry Bridge, and I thanked her again for a very good time. Greg arrived a short time after and took me to his mom's for some spoiling. Then we went to a local outfitter, where he got me a few more things. These support systems were key in my journey. We went out to a local eatery, and I talked his ear off about trail life and how freeing an experience it is. It was sad to say good-bye to him, but knowing I was crushing Pennsylvania pretty well without a zero-day was gratifying.

My next stop was the Darlington Shelter, where I decided to crash for the night. I was somewhat exhausted from the first ascent of only five hundred feet, but when the hike was so flat, that five hundred feet was like a thousand. I used the awesome privy there because it was, "Pooooopy Dooopy Time!" After I had eaten, I sat up and talked to Gilgamesh a bit. He thought I was going to be much farther ahead.

Eleven miles hiked into Duncannon the next day. I was feeling good, other than my first run-in with the bugs of Pennsylvania. They swarmed me right after my rocky descent into PA274. In Duncannon there are some cool spots for hikers to stop and rest, but since being pampered recently, I was good. So I continued on through the beautiful town. I crossed the familiar Clarks Ferry Bridge and over the Juniata River. The climb of Peters Mountain was nice. The sun was shining. A gentle breeze was in my face. I grabbed some water at the Clarks Ferry Shelter. As I was hiking out, I saw a man approaching me from the north, practically running.

"Hi."

"Hello, I hope you brought your bug spray. The bugs are really bad back there."

"I did. Thanks."

He asked no more questions but just continued hiking. My steps were quick. I felt the first few bugs dive-bomb my face. Although it was annoying, I did not bring out my DEET wipes my ma had sent me just yet. By the footbridge at PA 225, I had had enough. Thousands of little gnats swarmed and were in my nose, my ears, and my eyeballs.

There was a parking area at PA 225, and I decided after nineteen miles to call it a day. Once my tent was set up, I made dinner and walked around the area. To the south there were steps leading to a camp. I approached down the steps that said "no trespassing" and looked to see if anyone was there. No one was. On the porch there was a sign that read "By Fogarty." Did John Fogarty live there? I know what I was doing was wrong as far as the trespassing was concerned. But sometimes we do things we shouldn't. Plus, the view was incredible.

Pennsylvania for me was very nostalgic. It was a grueling summer. Sticky and hot were the ways I remember many summers of my childhood. My brain is sticky and hot sometimes. I can smell those kinds of seasons just by bringing the memory to live in my mind. Or I can recall a particular memory of the freezing waters at Sizerville State Park. It may have been summer, but don't tell that summer breeze. I remember many blue lips at that pool. Good times.

A quick pit stop at the Peters Mountain Shelter and the bugs did not let up their assault throughout the day. The 100 percent DEET wipes from my ma helped somewhat. When day turned dark, they relented a bit—a bit.

I made quick work of Pennsylvania hiking. The rocks always let me know they were there. It was usually my toe and a big trip up that alarmed me to their presence. If the trail had more elevation gains and drops, then maybe it could have been more tolerable. The toe hurts thrust me on in anger, and I thought to myself, "If a Uke curses in the woods and there is no one there to hear, does a Uke make a sound?"

The flat, rocky terrain led me past Lickdale, Pine Grove, and to the iconic 501 Shelter. This shelter is an enclosed hut-like structure with bunk beds and trail information. A trail hiker, named Machete, and others were there. He and I played some music by the fire while munching on some fresh fruits. He had a guitar, and I had White Blaze. He taught me some of the songs he knew and we had a grand old time.

Another hiker I had been hiking with, by the name Nomad, left with me from the 501 Shelter and along the twisty ankle rock scrambles into Port Clinton. The tough descent into the town did not make us happy. We both cursed loudly at the lack of maintenance in this section of the Appalachian Trail. We were heard by each other.

In town, Nomad and I walked the railroad tracks to the Port Clinton Hotel for a bite to eat. He decided on a beer, and in my envy, I opted for ice water. Their food there was okay. I got the Rueben and sweet potato fries. The two of us sat there, observing the local folks in their daily grinds. Observing our stinky asses was probably less than pleasant for them.

The pavilion was pretty full when we set up to sleep. We made happy music and imbibed on a flask of whiskey passed around. I indulged for a nightcap before saying good night. During the night, I tossed and turned. My feet and shins were sore from the tens of thousands of rocks. Although it was not the best night of sleep, I was making up the ground from getting held from the spider bite.

After waking up the next morning, many of us walked to a breakfast spot. The waitress was an older lady and was very kind. She served us all water before taking our orders. She was what I like to call "hiker smart." As the hiker band sat and ate on piles full of eggs, bacon, sausage, biscuits, and gravy, we were all smiling. Laughter happens when we close off the hose of negativity.

Nomad left to get a room in the neighboring town of Hamburg, and I waited for the post office to open. Ma had sent me some trail magic of tuna, cheese, Gushers, and other appreciated treats. I got my package and I got a ride to Nomad's motel, where he allowed me to shower. I was hiking out that evening and was hoping to get in around fifteen miles.

I said good-bye to Nomad and headed for a ride back to Port Clinton. A gentlemen driving a delivery van gave me a ride.

"I've never picked up a hiker before."

I crawled into his very limited space in the back as he drove on into Port Clinton. He dropped me off and wanted to get a picture with me. I of course obliged that kind of gesture. I also grabbed a picture with my camera. I thanked him and he wished me good luck as I began hiking back to where I got off the trail.

Chapter THIRTEEN

The hike out of Port Clinton was a steep ascent into overgrown briar bushes, hidden toe-hurt rock gems, and bugs. There was a group of kids near the blue blaze trail leading to Blue Rocks Campground. They hiked with me just before the sun was about to set. None of them had headlamps, water, or any food. They said they wanted to walk into Pulpit Rock View before sunset. I warned them they should have supplies for the mile hike in and mile hike out. They did not care for my advice and tried to keep up with me. None of them had packs on, and I pushed on far ahead of them.

I had caught a quick, colorful sunset before darkness overtook me. Pulpit Rock was only thirty yards off the trail. When I began hiking the thirty yards back to the trail, I heard the kids, who were behind me yelling. I thought about calling out to them to see if they were all right, but the experience is the teacher of all things.

The Elkville Shelter is a little garage shelter behind a caretaker's home. I made my way there and camped for the night. It was a very productive hiking evening. Inside the little garage shelter were three bunks. I expected to find some hikers there, but there were none. Alone I slept in the stillness and alone I felt accomplished.

A quick breakfast and an ascent of over six hundred feet made my morning. The sun was out, and the heat was rising. I knew what that meant, so I upped my pace to avoid the certain bug onslaught. By the time I hit the Allentown Shelter, I was already singing. "Aaaand I'm hiking near Allentown!" The trail continued its rocky ways with little to no elevation gain or drop.

I signed all the trail registers as I continued to Palmerton. The trail opened up from the tree line, across the Lehigh River, and into the cool little community. When I crossed the river, I looked up the road and saw a hiker I recognized.

"Peach Tree!?"

"Uke!?"

"What are you doing?"

"Thinking about getting off the trail, man."

"No way. You want to hike on with me?"

"I don't know, man."

"Come on, let's go into town. Then you can hike out with me later."

"I'll go into town with you, but I don't know."

"You're hiking out with me."

Peach Tree and I hiked into Palmerton and had ourselves some Chinese food, buffet style. We talked and laughed. It was good to see him again. Once we finished our food, we headed to a local park to digest and prepared our hike. A nice couple gave us a quick ride back to the trail. The rock cliffs that are the AT northbound out of Palmerton looked ominous both in the guide and to observe in person.

He and I hiked up the rock face early afternoon. I noticed there were no bugs, and I wondered why. Mainly because it was above tree line and also because we were walking on this little thing called the "Superfund."

The Palmerton Superfund:

The Palmerton Zinc Pile Site is the area of a former primary zinc smelting operation. The site encompasses the borough of Palmerton and surrounding areas, Blue Mountain, a large smelting residue pile, called the Cinder Bank, and much of the valley. For nearly seventy years, the New Jersey Zinc Company deposited thirty-three million tons of slag at the site, creating a cinder bank that extends for two and a half miles and measures over one hundred feet high and five hundred to one thousand feet wide. The smelting operations emitted huge quantities of heavy metals throughout the valley. As a result, approximately two thousand acres on Blue Mountain, which is adjacent to the former smelters, have been defoliated, leaving a barren mountainside. The soil on the defoliated area of the mountain has contaminated the rainwater flowing across it. The runoff and erosion have carried contaminants into Aquashicola (spelled correctly here) Creek and the Lehigh River. Approximately 850 people live within one mile of the site; the population of the town of Palmerton is approximately five thousand. The Palmerton Water Company has four production wells at the foot of Blue Mountain that supply water to the towns of Palmerton and Aquashicola; these wells have not been affected by contaminants from the site to date. This site was proposed to the National Priority List (NPL) on December 30, 1982, and formally added to the list on September 8, 1983.

When we arrived at the top of the Superfund, Peach Tree and I contemplated camping out there until another hiker came by and informed us of a festival that was happening four miles up the trail. It did not take us long to decide to hike on. The three of us arrived at the Slope Side Pub and Grill in time for a good dinner. The music was loud at the restaurant, but in the background we could hear the blues. It was the Pennsylvania Blues Festival at the bottom of the mountain. I wished they would have turned off the bar music so we could listen, but the management wanted their music to prevail. I thought they could have patched the excellent music through some blue tooth speakers from the festival to the bar. No big deal, as later we would enjoy it in the comfort of our beds.

As we sat there, Peach Tree had the idea to camp on the slopes so we could hear the festival below. In a way, I wanted to go down and get in the crowds, but I agreed to ask the manager if we could set up our tents somewhere on the mountain. It took her a while to get back to us, but she accepted as long as we camped away from the bar.

About a half-mile, we came to one of the chair lifts going up the mountain and set up our camps. The blues was echoing off of the ski slopes as we prepared for sleep. Once I was secure in my sleeping bag, I got out my phone and recorded what I was hearing. Magically lulled to sleep by the likes of Dumbstaphunk. It was a sweet lullaby.

During the night of our stay on the slopes, it had rained. Peach Tree had set his tent up in a dip and was pretty much in a small pond of water when he woke up. I heard him cursing as he was throwing his things out of his tent. Luckily we camped next to the sheltered ski lift where we were able to set our things to get them out of the rain. He and I chilled there for a bit before heading back up the hill to use the restroom and fill our water bottles.

He and I hiked back up the mountain to the restrooms. We waited as long as we could for the rains to subside, but it was going to be wet no matter what. The short road walk back to the trail led us across rock fields and eventually to the road leading to Wind Gap, Pennsylvania.

As we road-walked toward town, a 4X4 pickup truck pulled up to give us a ride. I threw my pack with White Blaze on the back. I heard the guy yell at us to get in the cab because it is illegal to transport people in the back. Before I could shout the information to Peach Tree, I saw him jump on the back. Seeing him fall on my pack was almost slow motion. I heard wood snap and break.

"No!"

"Oh, man, I am so sorry!" Peach Tree exclaimed sincerely.

"Jump in the cab."

As we drove into the town, the guy suggested a campsite a few miles away. Peach Tree was not keen on the idea, but me being the trusting sort, I agreed. Our ride drove us about five miles out of Wind Gap and through a huge mud bog. The truck leaped and jumped, slamming our heads into the truck's ceiling. I was in the front, and Peach

Tree sat directly behind me. I felt his fingers claw at my shoulders as our driver made it through the bog.

Once we were out, the driver pointed to an area for "camping." It was not much of anything, so I turned to him.

"There is some free camping at a place called the Beer Stein. Would you mind taking us back there?"

"This is a good spot; I'll come back in the morning to pick you all up."

"Oh, I am sure you would, but we would feel much more comfortable in town," I insisted.

"Okay, yeah, I can take you all back in town. I just thought you would like some privacy."

"I appreciate it, and I dig four wheeling, but we need to be back on the trail early, and I don't want to put you out."

Our ride repeated the mud jump back to the main road and returned us to the center of town. We climbed out of his monster truck and headed over to where several other hikers were sitting around the picnic tables.

I surveyed my much-damaged White Blaze. The side walls were popping out, but there was no damage to the neck as far as I could see. As the other hikers began making camp, I spent the next several hours holding the sides of White Blaze and applying copious amounts of super glue to the inside. The task was difficult, as I sat there thinking that after hiking with her for nearly 1,300 miles it had come to this.

With White Blaze drying, I began my ritual of setting up camp in the fenced-in area of the Beer Stein. Once I was done, I joined Peach Tree at the bar and had a shot of Maker's Mark to calm my shaky nerves. Peach Tree apologized profusely for jumping on my uke.

I said, "I think she will make it."

The next morning after packing up, we were about ready to head back to the trail when the Beer Stein owner came out to chat with us. He then offered to open his kitchen to us. We went back to his kitchen, and he explained that the Beer Stein does not serve breakfast. All the breakfast items in the restaurant were for us.

We immediately began forming a menu. Homemade guacamole, sautéed veggies, sausage, and cheesy eggs. A few tall glasses off OJ, and we were very contented hiker trash. I offered to help with the dishes, but the owner insisted that we did not need to clean up.

Peach Tree and I got our packs and headed out to the trail. A quick ride back to the trailhead and we were on our way. Halfway through our hike, we decided to take a break on a beautiful overlook. Peach Tree and I sat on a rock. I stretched my body back and over the back of the stone I was sitting on. I turned my head downward and was eye to eye with a black diamond rattlesnake. My body tensed up, and I heard Peach Tree say something about seeing a snake where he was sitting too. I inched slowly away from the now coiling, angry snake.

Safely I stepped away from the rock and grabbed my pack. I looked for other dangers at my feet. Peach Tree and I both exclaimed that it would not be wise to take a break where the sounds of several rattles were scratching our eardrums. I agreed, and we both walked gingerly up the trail.

A few miles away, we took a snack break and exhaled our relief that our friends did not strike at us. Late in the evening, we both made our way to the famous Delaware Water Gap, where several of my early hiker friends were hanging out at a comfortable and friendly church hostel. My trail parents, Blockade Runner and Hightide, were also there. It was a happy reunion.

With my bed in the hostel prepared, I washed my clothes and then my ass. Trail conversations were mainly about the amazing people at the Wind Gap Beer Stein, but also of how our bodies were changing. Many of my hiker family were commenting on the amount of weight I had already lost. I thanked them for their kind words. My trail friends are some of the best people on this planet.

The next morning I was one of the first people up. I met Zeus, a thru-hiker from Charlotte. He and I headed to a breakfast spot for a hearty meal before hiking out. Blockade Runner and Hightide were heading in when he and I were leaving. I recommended the SOS, and we laughed before heading back to the hostel.

I was ready to hike out, but I needed to wait for my new backpack. I walked around the quaint little down of Delaware Water Gap. I stopped and looked at the old buildings and observed a very proud community.

Later in the morning, I walked into the outfitter, and they indeed had my new backpack waiting for me. Once I replaced all my gear, I then put my tattered and very worn pack in the shipping box and slapped the return label on it. The outfitter was nice enough to send it out for me. The new pack was like putting on a brand new pair of pantaloons.

Peach Tree was waiting for me at the hostel, and we were ready to hike out. The road walk out of town took us to the Delaware River Bridge and Interstate 80. Peach Tree was behind me and called to me that he had forgotten something at the hostel. I yelled back at him and told him that I would meet up with him up the trail.

The Kittatinny Visitor Center was busy. Many day hikers were out hiking the well-maintained trails in the area. Several hikers were sitting at the base of the mountain. I approached them and noticed several large pizzas, a full cooler of beer, a full cooler of pop, and several sweets. Trail angels deliver. K-Biz, Schnitzel, Dutch, and the crew known as the Sun Gods were all laughing and shoving the goodness down their gullets. I grabbed a few slices, a couple of pops, and gave my thanks. A few minutes later, Peach Tree arrived and I was ready to hike on. He stopped for the goodness, and we agreed to meet up later on.

The thousand-foot climb into Sunfish Pond was very cool. The sun was shining the breezes were calming. As I was taking a spiritual moment at the pond, I heard Peach Tree behind me. We hiked together for the next two miles.

Kittatinny Mountain's cairn was huge on the summit. The grasses around the mountain were soft. Although he and I could have hiked on for bigger miles, the sun was about to go down. Our decision to camp on the summit for the night was a good choice. Miller Miller, a thru-hiker, also joined us on the summit for an epic sunset. We chilled around the cairn after setting up our tents. The three of us sat mostly quiet as the colors on the New Jersey horizon splashed across the sky. We all knew it was an all right experience.

Waking and moving the next morning was necessary. My goal was to be up before the sunrise to witness both experiences. I packed up before six a.m., sat and watched the sun come up, then yelled to Peach Tree that I was headed out. There was no noise coming from his tent. He was still snoring away the morning.

Stepping up my pace through forest and down a very rocky mount brought me to a footbridge and gravel road. A sign read, "Mohican Outdoor Center .3 miles." I wasn't going to stop, but I thought back to my work with the kids at another outdoor center in Fredericksburg.

The Rappahannock Outdoor Center is a very cool business based right on the river in Fredericksburg, Virginia. It offers kayaking, canoeing, river tubing, a rock wall, great outdoor education, and several team-building areas. The kids I worked with in the day school were lucky that they were able to experience the serene beauty of the river and the offerings of the center. One of the main reasons these troubled kids had the opportunity was in large part to a team-building company, called Elements to Excellence. I wore my E2E shirt for several hundred miles on the Appalachian Trail.

The kids were first taught basic communication skills through events, called initiative activities. One of my favorite activities that I participated in and facilitated was called mine field. A tarp with about one hundred divided squares made up a grid. The tarp would then be laid on the ground. The objective of the activity was to cross the boxed areas without hitting a "mine." The facilitator would line up the participants and explain the rules. Sometimes, to make the activity hard, a rule of "no talking" was given. The facilitator would have a paper with a replica of the tarp on it, also in a grid. The grid paper would have the correct "path" marked out on it. Each participant would begin and continue on the grid until the facilitator made a sound of a wrong box: "mrrop." The activity would end when each participant made their way across the grid without touching the mines.

Our clients would do these activities and work their way up to more advanced things, such as the rock wall. The rock wall was a favorite of many of our clients and one of many activities required to have safety harnesses due to the height. When I first began training for this program, I was unable to climb very far up the rock wall. After several years I would get better, and by the third year with the program, I was climbing to the top of the wall. The feeling was nice.

My passion was kayaking, and I always enjoyed working with the higher accelerated clients on the water in kayaks, canoes, and tubes. It was unfortunate that program was terminated, but the memories those kids and their staff had were mainly positive—unless of course people didn't like being in the water. That was a thing too. I, myself, was and am a water dog. Love me some water rushing, calm, falling, etc. If it is warm enough and safety permits, I am going in!

The Mohican Outdoor Center had a pretty stellar educational center and the grounds were very nice. There were a few folks hanging out there, but I did not stay long. I figured Peach Tree would be getting around soon and I wanted to meet him at the trailhead.

Chapter FOURTEEN

I left the outdoor center and began a pretty good pace. Peach Tree was sitting at the picnic table beneath the Catfish Lookout Tower. He said he thought I was a few miles ahead by now. I told him I had to stop at the outdoor center. After a few minutes, we took off again. The trail was pretty level and we just kept moving forward.

We arrived to Branchville, New Jersey, in the evening and decided to check out a bar, considering our positive experience with being treated well. The bar we went to had a sign out front when we approached: "Hiker Entrance." It led to the back of the establishment and seemed less than friendly. There were signs that hikers were not allowed to do certain things. It was not welcoming at all, but we tried our luck anyway. Our host sat us outside at some okay tables. I used the bathroom and went back to our table. The food was meh, so we finished up and donned our packs and left. He and I bordered on staying somewhere by the lake in town, but opted to hike a mile down the trail and camp instead.

Peach Tree got out before me the next morning as I told him I would catch up. Knowing our hiking styles, I knew that he wouldn't be that far ahead after I got it together. I took a little nap and woke up at around nine. I was moving slowly as I packed up. It began sprinkling a bit and my movements were a bit more deliberate.

The next shelter was a mile off-trail and I figured Peach Tree wouldn't stop there. So I hiked on quickly to catch up to him. I kept moving, step after step, faster, faster. Hours had passed, and I still had not caught up with him. Once I reached High Point State Park, I realized Peach Tree must have been behind a bit.

The next few days I hiked past several footbridges, quiet streams, and views of several beautiful lakes that are oddly named "pond." A quick stop in Unionville and I caught up with Hightide and Blockade Runner again. Zeus and I hiked together for a bit and he set a hell of a pace for me. We hiked together over hill and over dale. We ran down mountainsides, quite literally. Hightide and Blockade Runner were never far behind, and Hightide mentioned that Vernon, New Jersey, had a market with ice cream.

With the thought of ice cream in our brains, we were determined to make it there before they closed up for the evening. Zeus and I got to the footbridge and large field before NJ 94. He and I were practically running toward the red building with a big cow out front. Our breath was pressured when we walked in. They were still serving up the goodness. We grabbed ice cream and a bunch of fresh fruits. The back of the building had a nice seating area.

While we were enjoying our goodies, I said, "Damn, should we grab some ice cream for Blockade Runner and Hightide?"

"Yeah, I think we should."

Just as I was turning to go back in, I saw them running up the road toward the frozen dairy calories.

"That's funny that I thought of them and they would come running."

"Good stuff," I guess he said.

The four of us sat there on the back deck of this business overlooking a marvelous skyline from where we just hiked a huge day. We all decided to head to the church hostel in town and I was up for a day off. I hadn't had one in a long time and it was time. We left to go and hitched a quick two miles into town.

The Sun God crew was there, as well as an old friend I had not seen since Damascus, Virginia. I quickly settled into the small area when I heard, "Whisper's here."

"What? No way!" I shouted.

In Maryland, Whisper messaged me to "catch up." I just told her I would, not really thinking I could, but deep down I wanted to. The spider bites had held me up early on and I was hoping to catch up with several hikers I hadn't seen in a while. But Mailman and Whisper were two I really wanted to see and hug hard.

"Where is she?" I asked.

"In town."

Several of us decided on going out for pizza and I wanted to catch up with Whisper somewhere. It did not take long. She was in line getting food at another restaurant. I went up to her as she was walking back to the hostel. At first she thought I was some bum off the street. When she realized it was me, I think she was still a little creeped out. Ah, how I affect people. Whoops.

It was nice catching up with her and getting the trail news that Mailman was still hiking strong and I was almost within reach of my old trail brother. Whisper joined us at the pizza spot and we enjoyed good company and plenty of laughs. Whisper is a beautiful soul I enjoyed seeing around.

Vernon was a fun little town, and I was happy to have spent an extra day there. I was able to get myself clean and well rested before a trail friend took me back to the trail-head. And although Peach Tree had caught up, he decided to rest, as well. I gave my good-byes to everyone at the hostel and began my journey northward . . . to beer!

The first ascent was just under a thousand feet out of Vernon. Ten miles later, hiking by my lonesome, I hit the iconic AT white blaze paint with the initials NJ/NY. I snapped a quick picture, and off I went to the highest point on the Appalachian Trail in New York, Prospect Rock.

I met a few hikers along my New York sojourn. Some I knew well and some I didn't. My focus at this integral part was that of the laser beam. I hiked along lakesides and thick pine forests and saw amazing waterfalls. In fact, I was lulled to sleep by one, called Fitzgerald Falls. I hiked over boulders the size of large houses. I pulled and pushed myself through this rock formation, called "the lemon squeezer."

There was some talk of a few trail magic events that never occurred, but I was okay with that. The push forward. When I crested what is known as Black Mountain, there she was. At first I didn't know what I was looking at. The guide is what told me that I was looking at New York City. At that very moment, I said a silent prayer for all the good people who lost their lives on that fall September day. Sure, I shed some tears. Are you surprised by my tears? Good men also cry.

During my hike I also ran into Greenlite and First Gear again. We all were a lot stronger and most of what we were doing now was very much psychological. The three of us hiked to the top of Bear Mountain together. Bear Mountain is just about an hour drive from NYC. Many famous people hike in the area, but I couldn't care less about those kinds of famous people. The famous people I know are not regular famous people. They are seasoned, tough, sent through flames and ash, brought out the other side. The famous people I know are not on a television set. I often wonder if we all would just stop watching television for about ten years, would we even want to watch it again? Probably not is my guess.

First Gear, Greenlite, and myself found it a bit late in the evening to hike through the zoo. The Appalachian Trail for some strange reason white blazes through the center of the Fort Montgomery Zoo. Most thoughts of thru-hikers are the same. We just hiked 1,400 miles, seeing some of the coolest wild animals, and now this. For a purist hiker, the trail does close for business here in Fort Montgomery.

With the white blazes closed at the entrance of the zoo, we had two choices. Get a room in town or blue blaze around the zoo. Going around, or blue blazing, was not an option for me at this time in my psyche. So, it was decided we would go into the town of Fort Montgomery.

A gentleman and his young son, Josh, were heading to their vehicle when we approached them and asked for a ride into town. At first I think he thought twice, but at seeing the nice smile across First Gear's face, he accepted.

Not only did he take us to the grocery store and wait for us to shop, but he took us to the local hotel for our night's stay. We got our room and began making an amazing fruit salad in the hotel's ice and wine container. We feasted on the fruit salad and then roast beef and cheddar cheese sandwiches. The rest of the night was restful and introspective. Our digestion lulled us to a nice night's sleep.

Early the next morning, another thru-hiker, named Hump, was heading to the trail in a big pickup truck. He offered us a ride and we gladly took him up on his offer.

The zoo was open and we took our time watching all the trapped animals in their cages. They all looked well taken care of, but I am still not a big fan of zoos. The lowest elevation on the Appalachian Trail is at the bear den at 177 feet. The zoo workers were feeding the large animals fresh cantaloupe. I continued to hike through the zoo. The trail crosses over The Bear Mountain Bridge and over the rushing waters of the Hudson River. The wind was strong but soothing at the center of the bridge. I saw First Gear and Greenlite hiking toward me as I was standing into the wind overlooking the river. The smile on my face was enough to let them know how amazing my whole self felt at that point.

I stopped at the Graymoor Spiritual Life Center. I thought about staying, but there was a hiker there who would not stop talking. I mean, a mile a minute of incoherent words. I can do the same, but this was not what I needed. Plus Greenlite and First Gear hiked on. So I did too.

It did not take long to catch up to them. We would have hiked farther, but the skies became gray and began peeing on us. At Dennytown Road, there is a spigot on the side of an old pump building. I grabbed some water and began setting up my tent behind the information board. My tent was in some tall grass. Although it kept me pretty dry, this spot was not ideal.

Condensation formed on the side walls of my tent and I was getting pretty damp. I got on my knees and tried to avoid touching the wetness that formed on the sides. Once I was packed up and donned pack, I was on my way. I hiked alone through Clarence Fahnestock State Park and to the top of Shenandoah Mountain. I sat for a few minutes at this summit. On the rock outcropping was painted an American flag and a memoriam to those who died on 9/11/2001. I said a quick prayer to them. It is such an unfortunate smudge on our fabric. The condensation from my tent was now formed on the side walls of my brain.

I arrived at the RPH shelter and ran into my hiking pal from Tennessee. Mailman had arrived a few minutes after me. We hugged a bro hug like no other. Seeing him brought huge encouragement and positive uplift to me. Knowing he was still plugging away at this crazy adventure made all my doubts subside.

The RPH shelter was another "pizza delivery" shelter. Being so close to a major road helped in delivery drivers getting into the famous shelter. The large concrete refuge allowed for six hikers to sleep comfortably. Greenlite and First Gear decided to hike out. Mailman treated on the pies and I thanked him for the gesture. I decided to stay the night at the iconic spot.

The pizza arrived after Greenlite and First Gear came back. They decided to stay, as well. We gorged ourselves on the Italian goodness. Then First Gear brought out these waxy hollow things that go in one's ears to clear earwax. They both had a fun time clearing out the waxy stuff. I was always taught that earwax was a good thing. So, I opted out of that activity. It was not the first time I witnessed folks doing this.

Some of my coworkers from the day school I mentioned did an earwax clearing in the same way I witnessed First Gear and Greenlite doing. Funny thing, both times I saw this done, the people doing the wax removal laughed their heads off. It looked pretty therapeutic. I have to say, I have done this on my own head and have not laughed. It kind of burns a little. I did not like it.

The next morning the rains were a torrent. There was some drama with section hikers. I donned all my rain gear and hiked on. The rain continued as I hit Hosner Mountain

Road. The footbridge there was pretty cool and I just moved as quickly as my legs would carry me through the storm.

Interestingly enough, the next road led to a town, called Stormville, New York . . . fitting. I made my way to Pawling, New York. I had a nice conversation there with the mayor of the town. Pawling is very hiker friendly, and I was happy to experience the quaint, little town. A few teenage boys gave me a ride while the driver's mother was behind them. It was a little bit comical.

After they dropped me off, I headed over several stiles. Stiles are steps for hikers that allow hikers to travel over, but keep livestock in their respective boundaries. There are hundreds of these along the entire trail. I continued the journey through farmland, through wooded areas, and through two crossover borders with Connecticut. Until New York was in my wake.

Connecticut boasts less than fifty miles of Appalachian Trail, but the hiking is pretty stellar. The trail is mainly rocky with fewer mountains. I was hiking around Mailman. Sometimes we would be together and sometimes I would roll ahead. When we hiked in Georgia and the other southern states, he would whip my ass on trail. Here in the north, my legs were pistons, and it was nice to be able to keep up. There were many hundred foot climbs and descents through thick forests. Through muddy trail where some maintainers were nice enough to put down slabs of milled oak. An ominous river ford that almost had me swimming a few times. Another lemon squeezer-type section. The trail later falls from a steep drop onto a long, annoying road walk through Falls Village.

I met up with First Gear and Greenlite again as I was hiking into Salisbury. A lovely woman allowed them to stay at her house. We did not stay together long, as I was headed into town to the Scoville Public Library to catch up on my blog. I quickly wrote some horrible bit of prose and uploaded some pictures and then I headed to a neighboring town to do some laundry.

Midafternoon I was just about ready hike out when I passed a church with amazing drumbeats coming from the inside. "Oh what the hell," I thought to myself. There were about six people inside the small church, and I was welcomed to join in the drum circle. One of the participants handed me a drum and we began playing some pretty soulful music. I stayed a few hours before dark and kicked myself a bit for not getting back on trail sooner. It was so nice to meet the people and play the drums though. Live in the now; the moments are fleeting, so living now is key.

Hugs were exchanged and I made my way back to the trail just before I heard some grumbling from above. I noticed some flashes of light in the dawn of the evening. A thunderstorm was approaching and there was nowhere to take cover, so I began jogging. When I passed the place where Greenlite and First Gear had stayed, I thought about knocking, but figured I could get up the trail and set up my tent before the rains came.

No such luck, as the torrents hit just as I came to a covered parking area. "'Come in,' she said. 'I'll give ya shelter from the storm.'" I stood in an empty parking space for the better part of an hour, but the rains were not letting up and it was pitch black outside.

Reasonably, I set my tent up right in that parking space.

The morning after, I dried my things up a bit in the new sun. The partly cloudy day was welcoming as I climbed to the top of Lions Head with a view. Not too many hikers were around as I made my way to Bear Mountain, Connecticut, and down a sheer rock face to the beginning of a multitude of waterfalls.

Massachusetts welcomes northbound hikers with serene waterfalls and yet another rock face to climb. The summit of Mount Race was magic, as it had been a while since I was above two thousand feet in elevation. So were Race Brook Falls, gorgeous. A steep climb to the summit of Mount Everett and down into Guilder Pond. Three shelters after the pond were pretty much consecutive as the trail dropped into Mount Bushnell.

Chapter FIFTEEN

In Great Barrington, Massachusetts, I descended to town to celebrate walking from Georgia to New England with a New England staple: a warm, hot bowl of New England clam chowda with oyster crackers. It was delightful. For desert, I consumed five Twinkies and then asked around for a ride back to the trail.

There was a man leaving in a blue Dodge Ram truck and I asked him, "Think I could get a ride, please?"

"No can do. Sorry."

"No problem. Have a nice day."

The man began pulling out to the road about twenty yards from me when I saw his brake lights. Then his reverse lights clicked on. He pulled back to me and asked a few questions.

"Are you headed back to the trail?"

"Yes, sir."

"Hop in."

"Thanks so much!"

"My name is Joe. I see you have a ukulele. Have you been to the ukulele shop here in town?"

"Nice to meet you," I said. "My name is Lloyd, but they call me Uke. No, I am not familiar with this area. I didn't even know they had such a thing. My uke is pretty beaten up, though. Not much of playing anything elaborate at this point. I am carrying her to Maine."

"The Magic Fluke Uke Company is right up the road. I can take you there if you're interested."

"Well, yeah I would. Wow, thanks very much."

Joe pulled into the Magic Fluke Company Ukulele Shop. I got out and asked him if he wanted to come in with me.

"No, go ahead. They are really very nice."

When I walked in, I was greeted by a nice woman who noticed White Blaze, superglue and duct tape holding my baby together. We exchanged pleasantries and I explained that I was hiking the AT. She introduced me to her husband.

Phyllis and Dale Webb began making ukuleles in 1999, encouraged by Phyllis's brother, Jim Beloff. Jim is a musician and coauthor with his wife, Liz, who produced a wonderful book, called *The Daily Ukulele: 365 Songs for Better Living*. This book is a must for up-and-coming ukulele players. (I would meet Jim and his wife at the Richmond Ukulele Festival to get a signed copy of their book.)

I showed Dale White Blaze and explained that it had come from Georgia, without a case, by foot to his door. He asked about the maker, and I told him about Larry and his small ukulele operation in Stafford, Virginia.

"It sure does look like it needs some TLC. Would you like to me to fix it up a bit for you?"

"Really? Yeah, if you could. I would love that."

"Sure."

Dale showed me around the shop and introduced me to his son and other employees making the world a better place through music. He told me to look around as he began working on White Blaze.

The shop was very cool. It was almost like a living history of the ukulele. The ukulele was created in the late 1800s in Portugal. Later, the tiny, four-stringed instrument was brought to Hawaii, promoted and supported by King Kalakaua. Elvis Presley and TV also made the instrument famous. How fortunate I was to be in their ukulele shop along the Appalachian Trail. Their kindness to me was remarkable.

I watched as Dale finished up the tuning and played White Blaze a bit before handing her back over to me. Joe came in to take a few pictures of us. As I left, I thanked them again. Joe and I returned to his blue Dodge.

"Pretty cool, huh?"

"So cool. Thanks for bringing me here. Everything surely happens for a reason."

He dropped me back off on the trail, and I was headed north once again. I called Larry and let him know what had happened. She was still a bit beaten, but not out just yet. I also called my mom and a few other people who were supporting me along this journey.

The trail meanders over the Housatonic River before climbing to June Mountain. Continuing my hike with Mailman close at hand through the Berkshire Mountains was very charming. White oak, birch, and maple trees made up an expanse of canopy toward the best zero-days I would find on the trail. But first Mailman and I would go into the Cookie Lady's home and blueberry patch.

Unfortunately, when I walked across the street to see her, she was not in. A kindly older man explained she had prior engagements. I was sad that I wasn't going to meet her, but really sad that I wasn't going to get any cookies.

"I'm sorry about that, but hold on a second."

The man walked into the clapboard home and came out with a beautiful wicker basket. A white, ornamental doily, possibly handmade, draped over the basket and flowed on the outside. The man's fragile hand extended the basket toward me.

"The Cookie Lady is not here, but I do have some cookies for you if you would like. They're not fresh. Sorry about that."

"Oh, that is fine. Thank you very much."

"You're welcome. You can relax and enjoy your cookies here if you'd like. If you want to get a basket of blueberries, you can pick them yourself."

"I think I will do that. Thanks again."

The man walked away to take care of other customers. The cookies were crispy oatmeal raisins. They were good. I watched many people came to pick their blueberries and I was looking forward to doing the same.

The Upper Goose Pond Cabin is a half-mile off of the Appalachian Trail. Many hikers pass this gem up because it is "too far" to hike. Standing by the wooden post that informed me that the cabin was a half-mile off the trail, I also had this trepidation. Several minutes I stood there, arguing with myself the pros and cons the one-mile detour.

The cabin won out, and I hiked along the "pond," or as I like to call it, a "lake." The summer breeze was swift across the water. The ripples were forming with each gust. My mind was singing, "Ripple, in still water. When there is no pebble tossed. Nor the wind to blow . . ." I would fudge the words, but the message was clear.

A two-story red building situated right there on the water was in my view. I approached to find several hikers eating some beef stew made by the caretakers. I could smell the goodness as I walked inside. I walked through a small kitchen area, through the dining room, and the living room. Someone called out that there were a few bunks available upstairs. There were no open bunks, so I set my pack down on one of the top bunks and returned downstairs.

I met Chicken Man at an outside kitchen area that had a pavilion covering it from inclement weather. Many hikers were abuzz around the area, eating on their beef stew.

"There's no beef stew left; I'm sorry about that."

"Aw, man. That's okay, but it sure does smell delicious."

"Tomorrow we'll have some hearty breakfast though. Pancakes!"

"Thanks. I'm Uke."

"Nice to meet you, Uke. My name is Michael, but you can call me Chicken Man. My wife, Ruth, daughter, Ellie, and son, Carl, are the caretakers this week. Make yourself at home, and if there is anything I can do for you, please let me know."

"Thank you very much. I'll do that. I am sure I will be fine. I appreciate the hospitality."

"Talk to you later."

I made a dinner of shells and cheese with a pink salmon packet from my food bag. Wonder Boy and Piper also were present at the beautiful cabin setting.

The cabin grounds were impeccable. They had two canoes hikers had use of, primarily for picking up resupplies the cabin needed on the Lower Goose Pond, about a two-mile canoe ride away, and for fetching several jugs of fresh water from across the Upper Goose Pond.

The evening wound down and sleep came with vivid dreams of beer. I snapped awake a few times with the taste of some of that amazing dream beer. I grabbed my water next to my pillow, took a gulp, and went back to snoring . . . ahem, I mean sleeping.

I was up pretty early to watch the sunrise on the pond, as were several other hikers. I want to say that a triangle rang for us indicating breakfast time, but I don't remember if that was the case or not.

Blueberry pancakes . . . oh my. It was so good, and I thanked our hosts for treating all of us with so much dignity and respect. The family of four took a weekend out of their schedule to serve the needs of the very weary travelers. I downed my pancakes with strong, black, gour-to-the-met coffee. It was good to the last drop!

Ruth apologized to me that I was not able to get any beef stew the night before. I assured them that I was fine. In secret, she explained that it may be a good idea to take a day to relax at the cabin.

"Oh, no, I better hike out today," I replied quizzically. I was missing something. "Is there something else?"

"Yes. We're having an excellent meal tonight and I wanted to invite you and a few other hikers to join our family."

"Wow, I will have to think about it. But I am honored that you would include me."

Wonder Boy and I spoke about taking the canoe out early because they were going to be a popular recreational activity later on. Ruth asked us if we could canoe over to get water for the day and then to pick up the boxes of pancake mix at the adjacent Lower Goose Pond. We accepted and began a short hike to the pond's edge and wooden dock.

Wonder Boy and I paddled with Piper in the center of the canoe. A very cool south-bound thru-hiker, named FireFox, who canoed with Carl in the second boat, also joined in the water getting.

Wonder Boy and I had a difficult time getting in sync with one another. At times, we were headed backward, sideways, and any direction but forward. It took a long time and many loop-da-loops for him and I to work together in reaching the other side of the pond. FireFox and Carl were laughing their asses off at Wonder Boy and me as we made spins and circles before reaching them.

The water source was a shallow concrete pool. The jugs needed to be dipped in and then brought out slowly. So many jugs required filling, and we took to straining our backs to acquire the earthly fuel. After twenty or so minutes, we had the jugs filled and back into the canoes.

Piper and I continued the awkward style of canoeing until we were able to communicate better. We paddled over to the dock and yelled out to a few hikers to come down and grab the spring water. Once we dropped off the last off the jugs, the five of us headed to a large rock in the center of the pond.

We took the canoes around the pond and explored the niche. A canoe with two fishermen was also out, and we Yogi'd some summer sausage and other hiker goodness. Pond Magic! We thanked them and continued around the pond for a while.

A large rock protruded far above the pond less than fifty yards away from the cabin. We took our wanderings there. FireFox dove into the water from the stone, and we all jumped in and around the fresh, clean water.

The sun was warm, and the company was pretty all right. As we were having the best zero days of our hiking experience, the quiet of the day was interrupted. A powerboat came from Lower Goose Pond and approached our rock.

Piper did most of the talking, as some of us did not enjoy the disturbance of the calm. The motorboat people were pleasant enough, but I was happy to see them return to the other pond and out of earshot of our warm and pure rock.

Quite a few hours had passed by when we heard some people yelling to bring the canoes back to the dock so others could enjoy them, as well. The day was young, and Piper suggested we take the boats back for the others. FireFox and I wanted to explore the Lower Goose Pond and told the others we would return later with the ship. Carl, Piper, and Wonder Boy headed back to the cabin while FireFox and I pushed our upper body strength across the inlet from the Upper Goose to the Lower Goose Pond.

As soon as we entered the other pond, we realized it was much bigger than the Upper Goose Pond. A kayaker ran alongside us and pretty much challenged us to a race of sorts without saying anything. The kayak, made for speed, was doing a pretty good job of keeping up with us until several motorboats flew by, shifting the waters into small, two-foot waves.

FireFox and I used the waves as an advantage of downhill long strokes. As soon as we crested a wave, we would dig in hard and glide our paddles in the water. Before he and I knew it, we were running at an impressive speed. The pond was great, and we wanted to get back so our other friends could enjoy the lakes, as well.

Before heading back, we stopped at the Lower Goose Pond dock to see if the supplies had arrived at the cabin yet. We got out and explored the parking area, but did not see any supplies. Quickly, the two of us canoed back and pushed ourselves to the cabin's dock.

That evening Ruth made turkey, homemade cast iron stuffing, mashed potatoes, and gravy for Piper, Wonder Boy, myself, and her family. We sat at the table as many hikers observed. I felt a little sad that we were eating so well, but then again. That meal that day was an absolute perfect zero day.

Roadkill, Hawaii, Invictus, and Mailman hiked in late that afternoon. Roadkill also packed out a ukulele, and she sang beautifully. We all enjoyed listening to her play and sing. I played White Blaze a bit, but still had some practice to do. Roadkill taught me a few things, and I listened patiently to her lessons. With an amazing zero day behind me, I said goodnight to my weekend family and slept like a log throughout the night.

Chapter SIXTEEN

Once I peeled myself from Upper Goose Pond, I hiked out unyieldingly. The 20.6 miles into Dalton, Massachusetts, passed very quickly. A trail angel in Dalton allowed me to camp in his backyard. After I set up my tent and situated my sleeping arrangements, I headed into an Irish joint for some fish and chips.

A quick jaunt into Dalton, and I ran into Jolly Rancher, who allowed me to take a quick hiker trash shower. I sat around with them for a while, and someone mentioned that Mailman and Whisper were in the room next door.

I knew that my trail buds were right under my nose. I said my good-byes and thanks as I went to knock on Mailman and Whisper's door.

KNOCK! KNOCK! KNOCK!

"HEY! MAILMAN! WHISPER! IT'S UKE!"

A few moments later, Whisper answered and welcomed me in. I was happy to see the both of them again. I could tell they were settling in, and I was interrupting some sleepy time. Before I hiked back to my tent, I made plans for them to have breakfast the next morning.

I kept my tent up with my stuff inside so I could walk around without a load on my back. I met Mailman and Whisper for breakfast. We laughed a lot, ate well, and drank bountiful amounts of coffee. We talked about the plan to get to Maine, and I knew I would be seeing more of them before I ended this journey. We finished up, and I made my way to the library to update my blog. We agreed to see each other soon and hugged.

At the library, I finished the words for my blog and sent it off to my cousin. I needed to get to Cheshire for a resupply package. I was half-hitchhiking, half-walking the four miles to the town when a nice lady picked me up in her Chevy pickup. It was very sweet of her to take me to the post office, wait for me, and return me to my tent. The package from my cousins, aunt, and uncle was a bunch of trail goodness. I called them and thanked them after I packed up my tent to hike out of the small community.

My good friend, Ryan, was coming up from Pennsylvania to walk with me into Vermont. Plans were arranged to meet somewhere in North Adams, Massachusetts, the next day. I finished up my grammatical error blog and began to walk toward Cheshire.

The trail from Dalton crawls over Crystal Mountain. Then it goes down through the town I just left, Cheshire, and begins the epic ascent of the highest peak in Massachusetts. I could see Mount Greylock when I approached Outlook Avenue, a small stream, and a pipeline.

My feet were light with wings as I turned my pace to a staggering hoof. I passed more hikers going up to the peak than I have ever passed on the entire trail. Passing hikers, instead of them passing me, did feel pretty empowering.

The Appalachian Trail crosses two roads before reaching the summit of Greylock. Twice I thought I false summited, which means my brain thought I was there but my body wasn't. I ultimately did get out of tree line to see a huge building, called Bascom Lodge; I was encouraged. Beside the huge lodge was a massive structure that resembled a pawn from a chess game. I was in awe of the place. Across the skyline were epic sunset views of the Green Mountains of Vermont, Catskill Mountains of New York, and the Taconic Mountains of Massachusetts.

Piper and Wonder Boy were also there hanging out at the lodge, figuring out their next steps. Ryan and I were to meet the next day in North Adams, but being up on Greylock, I wanted him up there with me. I called him up, and he was only a few hours away.

After telling him my idea that we begin our hike on Greylock, he thought it was a very good idea and said he would be there soon.

Greylock is reminiscent of Clingmans Dome in that a nicely paved road leads from the bottom of the mount to the top and vice versa. I cannot express how annoying that is from a hiker's perspective, but I do understand. Mountains are fun to climb, but if some people are unable to, they're fun to drive up. Mount Greylock was a very positive experience.

Ryan drove up to the summit, and we met at the lodge. The clouds were sharing the sky with an explosion of stars and constellations. When we left Greylock to head to North Adams, Ryan rolled down all the windows.

"What's wrong? I don't stink."

"Ah . . . yeah you do."

"Well, I would much rather be warm than your olfactory nerves fall out."

Belly laughs ensued, but he still kept his window down.

Ryan got a lush hotel room and we walked down the hall. Ryan was behind me and he asked if I was alright because my gait was somewhat skittered.

"Are you ok?" He asked.

"Yeah, I just have a bit of a hiker wobble." I replied.

Ryan ordered pizza and took my dirty clothes as I lay naked in the hotel bed. He took great care of me but in the back of my mind I knew he was washing my things for his benefit as well. I guess I did smell a little musty. His experience with hiker trash was commencing.

Sleep came in and I was gone to the world sleeping on the cloud at the Holiday Inn in North Adams, MA. The next morning we had an excellent breakfast, and I prepared him for what to expect for the next two days. The trail from Mount Greylock drops an astounding 2,831 feet in elevation over six miles. This decline in height would be a chore. Ryan just getting from here with the lack of serious training on his part would prove to be interesting.

Brandi, Ryan's wife, his mother-in-law, Nancy, and their three lovely chillun (Enzo, Milla, and Aria) were going to pick us up in Bennington, Vermont. Then the seven of us would enjoy an awesome weekend together at a campground in Massachusetts. A concert was also lined up with a famous composer of some sort who wrote the score for a movie, called *Star Wars*[8]. Never heard of it myself, but I was looking forward to the hiatus.

Ryan and I returned to Mount Greylock. He secured a parking space for the week and off we went. The trail is steep and a bear on the knees going down. I told Ryan that if he needed to stop for any reason, he should let me know and I would crack him with a whip. I was jubilant he was out there with me to experience just a taste of what this life had to offer.

We paused for a breather and view at the summit of Mount Williams. We passed on a third of a mile side trail to Wilbur Clearing Shelter. A switchback trail and the straight-down, treacherous trail led us to Pattison Road and down across MA 2, where we took a seat in a yard right next to the trail.

There was a water hose we should not have drank from, but we did. I told him to hike on ahead for a while, and I would catch up with him. My pace was a bit faster, and going his pace was somewhat difficult for me. I knew the climb to the beginning of the Long Trail of Vermont (America's original long trail and the inspiration for the entirety of the Appalachian Trail) was going to test him.

---

[8] This may or not be LBS aka Lloyd's Bullshit.

Our goal for the day was the Seth Warner Shelter. Thirteen miles for his first day in this complex hiking section to me was damn admirable. Before we ascended, there was a nice water source we wish we would have researched before using the garden hose.

Ryan was doing great getting up to the Massachusetts/Vermont border. The eleventh state for me and the rest of the northbound thru-hikers. We stopped for a snack at the well-built Long Trail sign. I showed Ryan in the guide our camp destination from our current location.

"Are you all right hiking the next two miles? I think it would be good if I jumped ahead to set up camp. What do you say?"

"Ah, I think I can do it."

"Do you have your headlamp?"

"Yep."

"Are you sure you'll be okay getting there by yourself?"

"Yeah, I'll be fine."

"Are you sure?"

"Yes."

"Okay, I will see you at camp."

I bolted up the trail and noticed there was a logging road less than a half-mile away from the shelter trail. I grabbed out the guidebook, circled the area I was at, and wrote Ryan a note.

"Only a half-mile away!"

Then I dropped the guidebook in the center of the trail on a piece of dry wood.

I arrived at camp and saw what looked like a bus of tourists that were dropped off. The campground was full. The shelter was full, and I asked around if there were any tent sites available. Someone pointed to a side trail and said that there were a few left, "down there."

I thanked them and walked down the dirt path to two tent sites with plenty of room. I began setting up our camp and got out some food for us to eat when Ryan arrived. Invictus, Roadkill, Cheers, and Bones were camped twenty or so yards on the other side of the shelter. We started bull shitting for a while. I wasn't sure how much time passed when I heard from a good distance away . . .

"Uke!?"

"Yeah?"

"Someone is yelling in the woods!"

"What are they yelling?"

"Lloyd."

"Hey! That's me!"

I jumped up and walked toward the shelter trail entrance and listened closely. Cheers, Roadkill, Invictus, and Bones followed behind me then we all heard it.

"Lloyd!"

"Ryan! Ryan!"

"Lloyd!"

"Ryan!"

Cheers had on a full set of bright white long johns. The moon shone on him, and he did look like an apparition in the wilderness. With the very bright moon above shining on him, it seemed almost eerie. He, Roadkill, Invictus, and Bones all ran down the trail to Ryan. I had my camp shoes on, but I was close behind, as well.

My tramily found Ryan safe and walked him toward the shelter. He was explaining to me that the logging road had confused him. In the guide there is a road, so he thought he had passed the shelter. He circled back and forth and became a bit disoriented.

I felt bad that I had left my friend, but I was happy we were both in camp. He was pretty exhausted. I built a fire and made some butter and fresh zucchini from his garden in Emporium, Pennsylvania.

"I think I am going to bed."

"You have to eat something and drink at least a liter of water or you'll be dehydrated tomorrow."

"I'll be all right."

"No, man, you have to."

He took a few bites of food and drank some water at my suggestion, but I could tell he was not too far away from passing out. I apologized for leaving him. I was more afraid of when his wife found out. He exerted himself more than he had in a long time. The importance of drinking plenty of fluids and resupplying calories is huge in the wilderness. Keeping body temperatures in check are also important.

"Good night."

"Good night, I'll be in in a little bit."

I joined Roadkill, Cheers, Invictus, and Bones for a nightcap at their camp. I thanked them for hiking out to find Ryan. The trail provides even small rescues like that. It was getting late as I sat by their little fire. I wished them all a restful night's sleep and went to do the same.

Ryan woke up when I crawled into the tent.

"How are you feeling?"

"I'm feeling good, tired, and glad I made it."

"Yeah, me too. Hey! My ma sent me the *Cameron County Echo* in one of my resupply boxes. Want me to read it to you?"

"Ha ha, sure."

I began reading the newspaper from Emporium, Pennsylvania. It was as thick as the coupon section of the *Los Angeles Times*. Ryan and I started laughing hysterically at the writing style of the small town paper. It was our hamlet in the middle of nowhere. North Central Pennsylvania will always be home to the people who live there and for the people who decided to move away.

Ryan and I were up fairly early the next morning. We enjoyed a nice, hearty breakfast around the campfire. We agreed that Ryan would hike out first. I would get the tent down and clean up after our stay. This plan seemed pretty all right, considering the amount of people on the trail. It was like being in line at an amusement park.

Before Ryan left, he filled his water at the stream. He donned pack as I was sitting by the fire and I told him I would catch up with him later. I watched him hike back up the trail and enjoyed the fire and a nice hot cup of coffee.

In the climb out of Seth Warner Shelter, I expected for there to be dozens of hikers around me because of the many people who camped out the night before. I saw a few hikers as I ascended nearly seven hundred feet, but I assumed most of the people from last night were southbound hikers.

The trail went up and over the mountain, crossed a power line with a nice Vermont view, and went down into Roaring Branch Pond. That is where Ryan and several of our hiking family were taking a snack break. I made snack my first lunch with an MRE Ryan had brought with him. The tortellini in tomatoes and feta cheese was tasty.

Ryan left first again as I sat by the pond and took it all in. I dozed off on my pack for a little while but woke up about fifteen minutes later. I stood up stretched a bit and donned pack. The next few miles were nice. A climb to Consultation Peak, the descent across Stamford Stream, and I met several southbound hikers, Ryan, and our small crew.

We got water, made a second lunch, and had a nice time in the wilderness's three-sided Congdon Shelter.

Chapter SEVENTEEN

Ryan and I grew up together. He and his family were a prime factor in my not ending up in prison. My life as a stinking kid looked like it could go down that path. Ryan's dad, Greg, gave these inspirational words to me: "If you're going to be a bear, be a grizzly." I still consider those words valuable to me today. Ryan and I were also teammates. We were on both the wrestling and football teams at our school. There was a time in our adolescence when if you saw Ryan, I was not far away. It means a great deal to me that we are still friends and experiencing life vicariously through one another.

The last six miles from Congdon proved to be a bear for Ryan and his feet. In truth, when we got to road VT 9 and Ryan took off his shoe, it looked like chicken pox on his feet. Blisters are never a fun experience, and many hikers are unable to finish certain goals due to the nasty little puss sacks. Ryan would live and heal when he returned home. It was unfortunate that it took several weeks, but it was still sweet of him to come out and hit up those miles with me.

Ryan and I hitched a ride into Bennington, another first for him. We gorged ourselves on Chinese food, and Ryan sucked down multiple glasses of vitamin water while we waited for Brandi, her mom, Nancy, and their chillun.

It took some time giving Brandi directions to where we were laying in a grassy patch next to a church, but she eventually found us. The seven of us traveled back into Massachusetts for some pool time and a concert by this guy, named John Williams. He wrote some music.

The campground was calm when we arrived. Brandi made dessert in a Dutch oven over the coals of fire. The kids and I spent a lot of time in the pool, and we all had some good laughs.

The concert was at Tanglewood. There was a crazy amount of people there, but the music was nostalgic. That John Williams guy is a pretty good composer.

The last day we all drove up to the summit of Greylock to get Ryan's car. The views were fantastic. I am very happy they all got the opportunity to experience that with me. The appreciation I feel for not only these guys, but everyone who believed in me, was enormous.

Before heading back to the trail with Ryan and his son, Enzo, I gave the rest of the Emporium crew big hugs and thanked them again for an excellent time. Ryan, Enzo, and I had gone to breakfast before we headed back to VT 9, where he and I exited a few days prior. Ryan took a quick picture of Enzo and me on the bridge leading up to the Melville Nauheim Shelter. I began to hike up the trail and Enzo started running.

"I want to go with you!"

I had observed the root before his toe caught it and he went sliding face first about three feet. Enzo jumped up and started up the trail more.

"Are you all right?" I asked him.

"Yeah, I'm all right," he replied.

Ryan reeled him in to head back to Pennsylvania. I hugged them both and was sad to see them leave. There was no one on the trail I saw before going up the mountain.

Vermont was a muddy, rocky, and wet hike for me for the next week. I summited Stratton Mountain and the famous fire tower. Benton MacKaye stood on this mountain and dreamed in the 1920s of a trail spreading across the East Coast corridor. The wistfulness of the thing was breathtaking.

Mama and Papa Chip met up with me again in Manchester Center. They treated me to a delicious lunch and wished me luck as I hiked to the top of Bromley Mountain. There was a group of college kids there, and I stopped to complete a group activity.

"Hi, guys, would you mind doing something for me? I want you all to say, 'Ain't nobody got no time for that' as loud as you can, and I want to video it. Cool?"

Several of the kids were all for it, but I noticed some of them did not wish to participate in such a mundane task. Hey! The ones who did yell it out I thanked before heading back out on the trail. Before I knew it, though, I would be camping by another college group and they were so sweet.

I was relaxing in my tent when I heard someone say, "Are you hungry?" I replied quickly, "I could eat." The girl laughed and said there was some hot meal left over from the group. I told her I would be right out.

Some of the kids were getting a fire ready. Some asked if they could play White Blaze, which of course was cool. As the night wore on, we read aloud from two books: *The Hundred Acre Wood*, where a female student and I shared parts, and a rock-climbing book, called *Close Calls*. Another male hiker read aloud a story about John Long. That man was Mr. Insane-O when it came to rock climbing. I mean that in the most respectful way.

I bid my companions good-night and slept like a bug in a rug. The next morning I was feeling pretty spry. The climb over Styles Peak and Peru Peak were not effort-less, but somewhat exciting. A lot of trail maintenance was going on, and the trail was "closed" due to trail washouts from the quick snowmelts. I passed several trail crew and expressed gratitude for their critical work on the Vermont Appalachian Trail.

The hike out of the first road into Rutland was full of pine tree forest, a rock climb to a view of the Rutland Airport, a muddy trail, and a challenging, rocky ascent over the Shrewsbury Peak. Even more problematical was the climb to Killington Peak. I saw two hikers I knew southbound in a slack pack. I gave them a 'Uke pass,' like a hall pass, because they were some great hiker people. When I reached the blue blaze trail to

Killington Peak summit, there was Cooper Lodge. Sort of like the Blood Mountain Cabin on top of Blood Mountain. The rock building was built from concrete and mountain rocks. It was open to the elements, and I was not comfortable sleeping inside. Instead, I chose one of the tent platforms made from wooden slats just above the shrewd structure.

During the night, my camp was met with a torrential downpour and thunder and lightning at almost four thousand feet. A hiking pair had set their tent next to mine. Their trail names were Cannon and Lady Mac. They were very nice, and later down the trail I would share a very special day with them.

I packed up the next morning in the rain and made my way into the town of Rutland at the second opportunity for thru-hikers to get into the historic village. The hostel in Rutland was pretty full, but there was a bed available I took up quickly. The staff was very friendly, and cleanliness was an important priority for them. Every morning they dusted "everything.

Several hikers were there, and I was jubilant to see my old friend, Mailman, again. The last time I saw him, we had breakfast in Dalton, Massachusetts with Whisper. While I was talking to him, he said he was going to hike out the next day, and he wanted to know if I wanted to join him. I told him that would be nice.

The next morning Mailman and I were awake by five a.m. We sucked down some coffee and ate a quick breakfast. We thought we would get a quick hitch out to the trail from someone heading to work. It was pretty chilly outside when we walked toward VT 4. It was dark as we thumbed to every car heading our way. Before we knew it, the sun was coming up.

The two of us wanted to get an early start to kick up some Vermont dirt and get into New Hampshire. Mailman and I walked up the road and noticed a bus stop. I knew that the bus dropped close to the trail, so he and I jumped on the next transit bus with our overly large back packs and squeezed in amongst the "normals". I have never enjoyed being normal, but I appreciate those who choose that path.

Mailman and I climbed over five hundred feet to the Inn at Long Trail, but we didn't stop there. I heard great things about it. We did stay at Kent Pond and relaxed in the outfitters. From there we walked over Thundering Falls. The rushing waters were a peaceful sound as we stopped on the footbridge across Thundering Brook.

Mailman and I ran into a hiker, named Bills Bob, or that is what I called him. He had another name that I didn't use. The three of us hiked to VT12 and got a ride into Woodstock for a hearty breakfast. I munched on smoked salmon bagels and blueberry pancakes with real maple syrup.

The three of us relaxed in Woodstock under a clear sky and a warm sun. We went to an old bookstore and looked around. There was not a single employee in the shop as we sat and read for a while. The decision was made to hitch back to the trail and continue to New Hampshire. I quickly got a ride from a kind woman in a Mercedes Benz. When she dropped me off, she handed me twenty bucks and wished me well. I hugged her and thanked her for the gift before I got out. I waited for Mailman and Bills Bob to arrive before we all hiked out.

We hiked over Dana Hill, toward South Pomfret. The weather continued to be spectacular. At some point, we joined Lady Mac and Cannon for a few nights on the trail before we all hiked into Norwich, Vermont. We met up at a decorative pavilion on Main Street before the five of us walked to the Connecticut River and into New Hampshire.

We took our stinky hiker bodies to a fancy schmancy restaurant where Cannon told me he planned to propose marriage to Lady Mac at a special overlook somewhere down the trail. I thanked him for the information and said I could not wait to tell her the good news.

"That would not be cool," Cannon stated.

"I am not that coldhearted." I laughed

"Seriously, though, don't."

"Don't worry. Your secret is safe with me."

Lady Mac called around to find a place for us to stay. Some trail angels took in hikers, and she was successful in getting us a comfortable home for the night. Before being picked up, we all went to a bar that had the walls covered in signatures of hikers past. The five of us signed the walls, too.

Our trail angels picked us up and showed us enormous respect and kindness. We all slept on the finished basement floor. The following morning, there was some confusion on when we needed to leave. Our hosts needed to go to work. I was packed and ready while the rest my group was still sleeping.

"Is everyone ready to go?" our host asked me.

"Um, no. I can go and let them know that it is time to go."

"Yes, if you all want a ride, they will need to be up and ready very soon."

I ran downstairs and informed them that we needed to go. Groggily, they began moving and packing up. Our trail angel gave us a ride back to Hanover, where we had breakfast in an iconic little diner. Many laughs were exchanged as we sat drinking our coffee and eating our meals.

I needed to pick up a resupply package at the post office and told them we would catch up on the trail. After I had finished with my town chores, I began hiking north yet again up Lebanon Street, past the co-op grocery store, and into the New Hampshire forest.

As soon as I entered the wooded area outside of town, I noticed two hikers and a dog. When I got closer, I was surprised to see Lost-n-Found. She was with her hiker friend, Smiley501, and his dog. It was always nice to see hikers I hiked with in Georgia all the way up here in New England. They were still packing up and getting ready. I told them I hoped to catch up with them on the trail.

Mailman, Bills Bob, and I left the Ice Cream Man, Bill Ackerly's, home after saying our thanks. An AT concrete milepost was less than two miles away. Our ascent of over two thousand feet was quite impressive. The views from Lambert Ridge were an impressive open expanse of the White Mountains. I was the first to arrive at the Smarts Mountain Fire Warden's Cabin. Inside the small building was trash and foodstuff left behind by other hikers. It was not a neat thing to do. Something every hiker should know before heading out on any hike is very paramount. The acronym is LNT, and it means Leave No Trace. If any hiker packs out something, they should pack it out. There are cases where section hikers will offer to take thru-hiker trash out, but some folks just don't respect the environment well enough. Those people need more education for hiking in the backcountry. I cleaned up the area and put some of the trash in my bag to throw away when I got to town. Mailman and Bills Bob trickled in while I was climbing the unstable fire tower.

Smiley501, Lost-n-found, and Hot Mama joined our huddled cuddle puddle on the floor of the newly cleaned cabin. Throughout the night, it got a little chilly. The cold motivated me to be awake and ready by six a.m. The other cabin sleepers did not wake up as I left quickly down to South Jacobs Brook.

The pine needles were strewn forever across the trail and were comfy under my feet. I did not stop at the Hexacuba Shelter because it would have been over a half-mile round trip to get to there on the Appalachian Trail. The trail turned from soft pine needles to hard rocks. I was listening to my music quite loudly as I hiked to the top of Mount Cube. My hiker pal, Hawaii, was taking a zen break as I approached with my loud music. I quickly turned it off and apologized to her for the disruption.

She was very kind, and I left her to be in her peaceful mountain introspection.

The next fourteen miles were very awesome. I kept a consistent hiking speed and made Mount Mist faster than I expected. The descent from the mount hurt my knees, and I almost fell a few times. The thought crossed my mind that I had not fallen since starting in Georgia. Not counting a mudslide and jump up that was insignificant hiking into Pearisburg, Virginia. I have heard of people falling a lot. I arrived in NH 25 and took a long hitch into Plymouth, New Hampshire. The only reason I headed to Plymouth was because I wanted to check out the town where one of my favorite poets taught higher education. Also, I wanted to watch a foosball game at a local watering hole.

My foosball team lost, so I began walking out of town and back toward the trail. A nice young couple with their car packed up pretty tight picked me up and dropped me off a few feet from a where I got off trail prior that day. They wished me luck as I got out and I thanked them for the ride. I knew conversation at the hostel was going to be about foosball. My foosball team lost; I did not want to hear any chiding.

I opted to stay at the Jeffers Brook Shelter at the base of my next challenge. I crossed the footbridge and Jeffers Brook and ascended a little over a mile to the campsite. Other hikers were roaming about, getting water, and preparing for bed when I arrived. I did the same. My belly was full of bar food and cheap whiskey. My plan was to be up very early to tackle Mount Moosilauke at 4,800 feet.

Sleep came, and I was very satisfied the next morning. A large stretch and yawn as I slid out of my sleeping bag and then . . . bam! It was cold. I ran to get water for the day. Water was not going to be an issue for the day as there were three more sources on the rock steps to the summit of Moosilauke. I ran back to pack my bag quickly and hiked hard through the Pine Forest and above tree line. The exhaustive 3,400-foot climb was both monumental and meticulous.

The summit of Mount Moosilauke was splendidly cold and awe-inspiring. Here were several rock walled structures with several people huddled down in them to get out of the strong cold gust of winds. There was one of these structures not far from the summit sign that I used for cooking my lunch and getting out of the skin-burning wind.

Many day hikers asked, "Are you thru-hiking?" I would reply, "Yes." They would ask more inquiries that I would answer robotically. Weird that my enthusiasm for questions as the finish line loomed closer waned.

After putting some warm calories in my belly, I was packed up and ready to hike down the other side of the mountain. The trail was a muddy and precipitous decline of almost three thousand feet. At some places on the path, the rushing water of Beaver Brook made it slippery.

One step took me slipping over six feet. I felt like Nancy Kerrigan with my right foot extended above the ground while my left foot slid down the embankment. Just before I caught myself, there was a cliff. I grabbed a small tree and said a quick prayer that it would hold me. As I looked down to the manmade steps of old railroad ties, I caught my breath. Sweat was dripping off of me like a running faucet. My nerves were shaking my entire body. I cheated death, or at the least, a life flight off of that mountain.

My knees were a bit wobbly as I dropped into Kinsman Notch. Before I arrived at the parking area and bathroom, I looked down in the stream to see several dozen cans of a beverage I was forbidden to drink. Looking down at the hops and barley concoctions, from my home state no less, I was more determined than ever to continue beating my body up.

A day hiker had just come out of the bathroom when I appeared from the path.

"Are you headed into Lincoln by chance?"

"Yeah, do you need a ride?"

"I would love a ride, yes, please."

He took me into town and dropped me at the post office, where I was expecting some trail magic from my ma. I showed my gratitude for the ride and he drove away, wishing me luck. A trail angel in town converted his home into a sweet hiker bunkhouse. I left the post office and headed toward his house.

When hikers arrive, he asks three important questions to separate the riffraff. I was not different when I first arrived. Chet came out and asked me:

"What mountain did you climb to get here?"

"Moosilauke."

"What mountain will you climb when you leave?"

"Kinsman?"

"And where did you hike from when you began?"

"Georgia."

"You did good, but you got one wrong."

"I did? Which question?"

"The next mountain you climb when you leave here will be Mount Wolf. Welcome. Make yourself at home."

"Thank you."

A rite of passage was complete for me as Chet began telling me the ins and the outs of staying at his home. After the tour, I grabbed a bunk and made myself comfortable. Several hikers were there, and it was so good to see so many of the people I had hiked with from Georgia, Tennessee, and North Carolina. The trail is a peculiar place, but one of mostly love.

I walked into town to a fast food restaurant I hate, but I ran into Mama Chip, who was updating her blog on her computer. She and I sat together updating each other on trail happenings. Chipmunk was due back and running behind. I was confident in Chipmunk, but the disaster I averted coming down from Moosilauke had me worried. I tried to reassure Mama Chip, but I probably made her more nervous the more I spoke. Moral of the story: I should speak less.

Chipmunk did not finish until late in the evening and Mama Chip did call the authorities to give them a heads up on her daughter not making the checkpoint in time. I was worried for her, but when I received a text from them that she was safe, all was right with the world.

Chapter EIGHTEEN

I slept well the night before, but I learned a friend had lost his mom to cancer. I spoke to him via social media and told him I would dedicate my day's hike to his mom.

The hiking from Kinsman Notch continued on a mud-and-stone riddled mess of a trail. Mount Wolf had an impressive view. The sky was partly cloudy, and the sun was warming me up. From Mount Wolf, the path falls into Eliza Brook Shelter, where hikers Smiles and Smirks met up with me as I was having lunch. The two were a hiking pair that were fun to be around. After my meal, I continued an ascent of the south and north peaks of Kinsman Mountain.

From the summit, I could see some clouds coming in, and at 4,300 feet, I did not want to stick around to see if there was moisture in them. I said several prayers for my friend's mom at both Kinsman summits and hiked down the rocky cliffs toward the first hut on the trail.

The words for protective structures are different throughout the trail. Some are called shelters, some are referred to as huts, and some structures called huts are high buildings with many amenities. New Hampshire boasted this phenom in the woods. The "huts" were equipped with kitchens and a group of workers, called the "Croo." There are no roads into the building, just footpaths. Helicopters bring in the Croo's necessary supplies. The whole thing is pretty damn amazing.

The steep rock steps leading to Lonesome Lake Hut for me were disastrous. I mis-stepped and smacked my kneecap into a boulder the size of a small car. I could hear hail slapping the rocks behind me as I was racing away from the little sharp pebbles of ice. My foot caught a root ball and pushed my leg forward into the boulder. I screamed out in pain. I stopped there and assessed my old foosball knee. It hurt bad, and I was bleeding a bit, but I could still limp.

My intention was not to stay at the Lonesome Lake Hut, because I wanted to head back into Chet's for another relaxing night's sleep. When I limped into the beautiful structure and fantastic lake view of Lonesome Lake, I had the decision to make.

In New Hampshire, the lead Croo member can take a certain number of thru-hikers in for the night. The hikers ask for "work-for-stay"[9]. Sometimes the work is difficult and other times it is as simple as sweeping and putting up chairs. I was sitting outside on a bench putting some ointment and a Band-Aid on my knee when one of the Croo members came up to me.

"Are you looking to do work-for-stay?"

"Yeah, if it is available."

"It is. When the paid customers eat, we'll call you in. We'll give you a small chore and then you can eat whatever is left over from dinner."

"Thank you for that."

My chores lasted less than ten minutes, and I asked if there were anything else I could do. The lead Croo member said that everything was taken care of, but if I wanted to play some music for the hut, that would be great. I played White Blaze some with a Croo member who had a mandolin. I sang an Appalachian Trail original, called "Get Outta Here, Bear!"

Thru-hikers usually do not get a bed to sleep in because of the other guests who pay a pretty penny to stay. My bed was on a bench, and I had a comfortable night's sleep.

---

[9] Work for stay is pretty much what it says. Get a chore list, finish the chores, sleep, and in many cases eat a fabulous home cooked meal.

My knee was feeling sore the next morning, but I had the full range of motion. That was a huge plus for hiking out unencumbered. With my bag once again packed and ready, I gave my appreciation to all the workers of Lonesome Lake Hut and made my way down to the water's edge of Lonesome Lake. I stood for several minutes looking up to my next challenge: Mount Lafayette and the Franconia Ridge. Looking back at the Kinsmans, I realized that Mount Lafayette was not much steeper. That gave me hope.

The trail meanders along the lake for thirty or so yards until it crawls into the forest and down along Cascade Brook. The Croo told me about the bridge being out, and they said I would need to ford somewhere along the rushing creek. When I came to the sign that said what the Croo had told me, I began searching the banks of the water to find a safe place to cross. I was not excited about the outlook. Many locations in the water I could not tell the depth. I contemplated taking off my boots, but felt I would have better stabilization with them on. Using my trekking poles, I checked the water as I made my first attempt.

The water was pushing hard against my sides when I took a few more steps. My instincts took over, and I climbed back out, fearing I would fall in and down several steep waterfalls below. I stepped back up the bank and hiked upstream. I found a deeper section, but the water was less cagey.

I dropped in with my hiking poles in front of me. The water went up past my waist as I made my way across to a protruding flat rock. I climbed and made a big leap to another rock on the opposite bank. I realized I was safe, and that made my nerves a bit less crazy. However, I was nowhere near the trail, and when I began the trek back downstream, I noticed there was yet another rushing creek in front of me. This crossing was just as sketchy as the last. I repeated the long process of crossing the water yet again. With gumption and determination, I flew my body through a deep, high torrent of a creek. Again, safe. I needed to find the trail.

I walked through thickets of brush. Then I heard voices calling out toward me. They were not talking to me, but I noticed they were far up on the ridge about thirty or so yards. What was supposed to be a mainly downhill day turned out to be me clawing earth hand over hand up a steep side hill to reach the Appalachian Trail. With my feet on solid AT dirt, I felt a bit better, but somewhat worn out physically, I pushed on.

The trail popped out at US 3 and an underpass for Interstate 93, where I got a ride from an older gentleman listening to some Merle Haggard. When I got to Chet's place for my second stay, there were even more hikers who came in. Bills Bob and Hawaii were among them. The three of us made arrangements to have a couple trail angels' drive us back to Franconia Notch.

Franconia Ridge loomed in our minds as we climbed the rocky New Hampshire steps to Liberty Spring Campsite. We all did some water getting before the caretaker at the campsite came over to where we were about to hike out.

"Are you all planning on hiking on?"

"Yeah," said Bills Bob.

"I would advise that you not. There is a bad storm about to hit the ridge within the hour."

We all looked at each other. Hawaii turned a bit pale and I may have, as well, before Bills Bob looked at me.

"Do you think we can make it?"

"I'm willing to try if you are."

"I think I am going to stay here," Hawaii stated.

I stood there with my pack on my back, silent for a few seconds, realizing I was wasting valuable time making a decision.

"Yeah, I think we can make it."

"Let's move then!" Bills Bob said and started north.

"Be careful!" the caretaker called out to us as we said farewell to Hawaii.

"Bye, Hawaii. See you tomorrow!"

Bills Bob and I were moving at an alarming pace. The sky above us was still blue with big, white puffy clouds. I was confident we were not going to see any precipitation by the looks of things. When we rock climbed out of the tree line over Little Haystack Mountain, my concerns were nullified. We could see the first two ridges of Mount Lincoln as we traveled along a narrow path that, to the right and left, fell down several hundred feet to rock fields below. The sky to our right was picture perfect. The sun shown bright and the sky remained blue with patches of large white puffy clouds. Then a frightening image came down with a crack from our left side.

"Holy shit! I yelled as I turned to Bills Bob.

"What do you think?" he said.

"I think we better run."

"I agree."

Clouds of an array of grays loomed to our left like a rolling pin of destruction. We could see it moving slowly from about forty yards away just a half-mile to the summit of Mount Lincoln. The winds were fierce on the left side of our bodies. It took strength pushing ourselves against gusts of wind to keep upright. We then moved up the ridge, where I saw several more strikes of lightening, and the thunder was deafening. In between boulders, the wind was whipping the clouds across the crest like a dozen racecars passing spectators at a NASCAR event.

The rains came first in a mist, then in spit, and finally, the sky opened up a can of whoop-ass on us in the form of rain and hail. The temperature dropped a lot when we stopped by a rock the size of a house. The two of us crawled underneath of it for some protection from the moisture but not the chill in the air. On the ridge, there were no comfortable places to set our tents. We sat there under that rock, each of us with racing thoughts.

"I think I am going to stay here," Bills Bob said.

"Here? I don't know, man. My thought is, we are going to die one of two ways: lightening or exposure. I am going with the first choice. I am getting the hell to Green Leaf Hut."

With that last statement, I was gone. Green Leaf Hut, unfortunately, is 1.1 miles off of the AT. That is over two miles round trip of extra hiking. Had the weather cooperated, I would not have gone down. It felt like forever climbing to the summit of Mount Lafayette. Bills Bob caught up with me and passed me in a sprint.

Each of us showed fatigue as I crouched down to be the lowest point on the ridge. He turned and looked at me crouching down. The next thing I saw was him crouching down. The both of us were competing for the lowest point on the mountain. Cheating death with each increase in elevation as the cold wind and storm raged harder around us.

"Tell my family and friends I was happy. You know, if I don't make it."

"Yes, same here. If we both don't make it, though, what then?"

"I hope they know. Yeah, I think they know."

The clouds hid the verity of us being on the summit. I heard him call out a few yards ahead.

"We're here; the Green Leaf Hut is down there," Bills Bob said, pointing down a side trail.

We could only see a few yards ahead of us. The ascent to Green Leaf Hut was a bear, and my knees felt every rock and stone. One point one miles seemed like an eternity, but the more we dropped in elevation, the less we were in the crux of the massive squall. A quarter of a mile later, we were under the storm clouds we just left with a small window down to observe the high hut of Green Leaf.

The arrival at the hut was triumphant. Bills Bob and I decided to add a little levity to our shaky nerves. I knocked on the door to the hut.

"Come in," said a voice inside.

Bills Bob and I walked in, sopping wet with serious looks on our faces. About a dozen people were sitting at the dinner table munching on some hut goodness. The smells of the inner sanctum were invigorating.

"Do you all have Wi-Fi here?" Bills Bob asked quizzically.

"No," said one of the Croo members.

I turned to Bills Bob, and he turned to me. On our heels we turned back to the door and left the building and stood just outside. We heard large bits of laughter in the spacious room before heading back in.

"Do you all have work-for-stay?" I asked.

"Come in, get out of your wet clothes, and come and join us for dinner," the smiling Croo member welcomed.

"Thank you," we both said.

Smiles and Smirks were there, too, and they stated that they had just beaten the storm before heading down the mountain to the hut. I was happy to see everyone safe and didn't expect anyone else due to more storms in the forecast. We probably should have listened to the caretaker back at the campsite, but that experience was pretty friggin' awesome.

Dinner was homemade split pea soup with ham and homemade pizza with fresh vegetables, and there was fantastic company to boot. Our hosts treated us with the utmost respect; the camaraderie of the trail was alive and well.

The next morning was cloudy and overcast with a soft mist spraying the rocky mountainside. I thanked the Croo for an excellent time. Smiles and Smirks were planning their day as I was leaving.

"I'll see you guys at Galehead Hut, right?"

"Yes, we will be there," Smiles assured me.

"See you then."

I left about thirty minutes behind Bills Bob, but I had no plans of catching him. I was going to the next hut, and I was pretty sure he was going to try to make it to Zealand Falls Hut. I was taking my good old time in the gorgeous White Mountains. I was looking forward to the Presidential Range, but they were going to be there when I got there.

The hike out of Green Leaf Hut sucked hard. I was not a fan in the least of climbing the rock steps the mile point one. I was not a fan of it, not in the least. I had taken a few breaks before I approached the Lafayette Summit. Standing at the sign that reads "5,263-foot Mount Lafayette," I still had no view because of the cloud cover, and I was disappointed in that fact.

The descent into Garfield Pond was a knee biter. I was moving at a good pace when I arrived at an intersection for the blue blazed Garfield Trail and the Appalachian Trail. The sign pointed down the mountain, stating that was the way to hike to stay on the AT. I didn't stop and read it for an extended time as I wanted to keep moving.

I was heading down several switchbacks and had gone about a mile and a half when I approached a southbound hiker coming toward me. Well, what I assumed was a southbound hiker.

"How far till the hut?"

"You're headed to the trailhead and the road."

"Wait—I'm going the wrong way?"

"Yeah, you are if you are heading to Galehead. I am the caretaker at Garfield Ridge Shelter."

"Thanks. Running into you was a real thing. See you up the trail."

I nearly took a sprinter's stance as I turned on my heal and leaped the mile point five back to the sign I should have stopped and looked at more carefully. Bills Bob played a little prank on me, and I laughed hard at the setback of three miles. I may have thought he was a bit of a jagoff before we cheated death together, but no, he is a jagoff.

Before heading from the Garfield Trail to the Appalachian Trail, I made a point of moving the sign back in the correct position. I made my way down the steep, rocky steps until I came to the sign for Garfield Ridge Shelter. I thought of my friend who was behind me, but saved me from hiking to the road. From the left of the trail, a (most times) small stream follows down in a cascade. I was only twenty yards past the trail entrance when I looked down a cliff of cascading water. The trail had literally become a waterfall.

With nowhere else to go on either side off the cliff, I was stuck. Bravery stepped in for a moment as I did step into the rushing water. The water was only four feet across in length, but the water was pushing on the backs of my calves as I made two sliding steps to the first rocked stair. When I took my foot down, the water was now near the bottom of my buttocks. I looked down fifty feet and said, "No way, man!"

I jumped out of there and hiked up to the Garfield Shelter. Several other cool hiking pals were also there. Smiley501 and Lost-n-Found were there when I came into the building with a tree growing through it. The caretaker asked for the overnight fee of eight dollars from everyone, and we kindly gave it to him. He offered us receipts, but most of us did not want the added weight.

Critter and Boomerang came in, as well as Hawaii. Hawaii was glad to see I made it through the storm still somewhat healthy. My thoughts in the shelter were of Smiles and Smirks. I realized I did not make it to them, and I was disappointed. Also, I was concerned about them. Had they walked down the waterfall, or was it a bit calmer water when they descended? These were my questions, but out of my racing thoughts, the caretaker asked a question.

"Would anyone like any hot tea?"

"Sure, I could murder one."

"There won't be any murdering around here, let me tell ya."

"Nice. Yeah, I will have some."

We sat and had hot fluids while the misty rains were intermittent in the White Mountain Wilderness. A mention of a chilly forecast and I was all ready to crawl into my sleeping bag. Boomerang slept next to me, and I noticed she did not eat that much.

"Can I make you some oatmeal?"

"No, I'll be fine."

"What I meant to say was, I am going to make you some oatmeal."

I put a half of cup of water in my stove and brought it to a quick boil. It is very much frowned upon, the cooking in the shelters. My friend needed to eat and Jennifer happened to send along these fancy oatmeal packages. They were much better than the packet sort.

"Here ya go."

"Aw, thanks, Uke."

"You're quite welcome."

Sleep came pretty quickly, but the weather outside did not sound excellent. The cold rains continued to fall throughout the night. There was not a free sleeping space inside, and that was good for all of the body heat that was being dispersed throughout the mostly enclosed haven.

I woke up and walked down to the cascade to see if it was safe enough to descend. When I saw the water higher than when I stood in it the evening before, I became convinced at that moment that Garfield camp was going to be a zero-day shelter. I made my way back to the shelter and told the hikers there the bad news. One of the hikers I was not familiar with was going to attempt the waterfall descent.

Lost-n-found, Hawaii, Smiley501, Boomerang, Critter, and myself all agreed that we would relax in the safety of our Garfield home. Throughout the day we ate well, played shelter charades, and sang songs. I sang a song my friends, Bobby and Claire, used to sing, entitled "Beer." I asked my shelter folks to sing the word "beer" in time. Like . . .

"Beer . . . Beer . . . Beer . . . Beer . . . " Etc.

Then I would sing these words: "Beer . . . Beer . . . I love Beer/gonna get me a tall glass of Beer . . . Beer . . . Beer . . . Beer . . . Beer . . . gon-na drink a lot of Beer . . . Beer . . . Beer/I'm gonna have a frothy glass of Beer . . . Hops and Barely are my friends/gonna drink Beer till the bitter end . . . Beer . . . Beer . . . Beer . . . Beer, THE END!"

The day's shelter zero was an absolute success. Great company and ready for a ten or so mile hike planned for the next day. Another full house that night brought the welcomed body heat. I shared some of my aunt's now famous homemade strawberry fruit roll-ups. Then I ate a nice supper, brushed my teeth, and fell fast asleep.

The next morning's weather was better with the sun peeking in here and there. The clouds were still hovering, but not pissing on my head. The stairs that were the waterfall the day before were now just a trickle of a small creek. There were some rock crawls and root pull-ups getting to Galehead Hut. As soon as I rounded the corner, I was in awe. The building was perched on a mountainside with an epic view of South Twin Mountain. I walked in to speak with the Croo. They allowed me to do some dishes for a healthy and hearty lunch. I asked if they minded if I charged my cell phone and accepted that "No. Sorry, but the solar has obviously not been giving us much. We need to reserve all we can." I responded with, "No problem."

Critter and Boomerang came into the hangout and ate some good hut grub with me. They were good company, and I was happy to see them again since hiking together in Tennessee. The two of them had been walking together for a long time. It was not long after I finished eating that I went outside to enjoy the rays of the sun. Critter and Boomerang said they would see me later. I said, "Good luck, be safe, and I will see you both soon."

While I was sitting on the front porch of Galehead Hut, a young woman was out front in a flat area doing yoga. Her talent for yoga was impressive, as she was moving her body in positions I have never witnessed any human body do in my presence. When she was done, she walked up to the porch.

"That was incredible. How long have you been doing yoga?" I asked.

"About ten years. Thanks, it took me a long time to be able to make those moves."

"You picked an epic location for it."

"Yeah, this place is magic."

With that I never saw that woman again. She was inside talking to the Croo when I donned my pack for the thousandth plus time and headed up a steep one hundred-foot climb to the summit of South Twin Mountain. Another mountain above the tree line that opened up my senses to the vastness of our lives . . . of my life.

I saw an American flag sticking up out of the Earth as I crested the other side of the mountain. The breeze was much stronger on the north side. The gusts were taking my breath away as I descended into the Guyot Shelter trail sign. The sign said the shelter was over a half-mile away, and I was not interested in hiking there. I already took a three-mile detour a few days prior. I was kind with the extra steps.

The next three miles was an almost 1,900 feet in elevation drop into my next hut stay. Zealand Falls Hut is another prime location for a respite in the mountains. As I arrived, the Croo was busy preparing dinner for their guests. I asked about work-for-stay, and they did have an arrangement for me. I needed to wait outside until they called me in, and I was okay with that.

I took the time to wander the grounds and observe the waterfalls just to the right of the hut. A magnificent view of Crawford Notch and Webster Cliffs loomed in the far distance. The euphoria was spine tingling.

"Uke?"

"Yeah?"

"You can come in now."

"Thank you."

The Croo let me feast on their homemade goodness before doing some chores for them. So far in every one of my hut stays, the Croo employees had been 100 percent kind and thoughtful of me. I did hear of some instances where hikers needed to be turned away from the huts for whatever reason, but I did not experience the issues of not having enough space or whatnot.

Chapter NINETEEN

With Zealand Hut behind me now, I made a good time along a steady, well-manicured trail to Crawford Notch and US 302. My supplies of food were well stocked, thanks to an incredible support system. But as I was standing there, thinking of what was up the trail a mere thirteen miles, my body cried for another day at Chet's. My brain agreed, and I stuck out my thumb to a very limited number of cars driving back into Lincoln.

It had taken less than fifteen minutes before I was welcomed by a kindly gentleman from Lincoln. He dropped me off at Chet's, and I went into a bunch of hikers who were at different spots along the trail. I got a bunk and talked with a few hikers regarding all things Appalachian Trail. The time with people attempting the same goal was motivation enough. My taste buds were slapping the next reward of that hops and barley liquid.

I spoke to Mama Chip about a possible ride to the trailhead the next day, and she and Papa Chip were happy to take me. I would also be in the company of two other hikers and their dog along the 5,011-foot climb to the historic Mount Washington. Mama and Papa Chip agreed to pick us up at Chet's early the next morning. I thanked them and had the benefit of a peaceful night's sleep.

The next morning I felt good. The advantage of rest, with plenty of fuel in my system, was a positive combination for the day's climb. The Chip-mobile dropped us off at Crawford Notch. Several hugs and words of encouragement were exchanged as Lost-n-Found, Smiley501, and Hot Mama hiked off into the forest just before a demanding ascent of Mount Webster.

I was soaked with sweat, but we continued to Mitzpah Spring Hut and Nauman Campsite. As we approached, Smiley501 said he needed to check on a campsite because his dog, Hot Mama, would not be allowed inside the hut. I told them I would catch up with them later.

The Croo in Mitzpah Spring Hut were busy when I entered.

"Can I speak to someone about doing a work-for-stay, please?"

"Hold a few minutes. Can you have a seat?"

"Sure. Thank you."

The hut was very busy with many customers, and I was afraid they may not have the position due to space constraints. I thought wrong.

"Hi. Were you looking to do work-for-stay?"

"Yes, if you have it available."

"Are you thru-hiking?"

"Yes. I left Georgia in March, got bit twice by a brown recluse spider, and now I am here."

"Oh my! Yes, we do have some work for you to do. Come with me."

She took me to the kitchen, and I began working on dishes and sweeping up the dining room. As I was working, the other guests were eating a hearty dinner of homemade bread and lasagna. The whole hut smelled divine. I was ready to eat, myself. Not me eating myself, but I was willing to eat food.

"You did a great job. Thanks. Help yourself to the food laid out in the kitchen."

"Thank you all so much. I know you all are really busy. If there is anything else I can help—"

"No, you are good. Eat your fill and find a spot in the dining room to bed down for the night."

"That is awesome! Thanks again."

The next morning, Lost-n-Found, Smiley501, and Hot Mama got out on the trail before me. I was asked to sweep up after breakfast and was waiting for the other guests to finish up eating. One of the Croo members saw me talking to Lost and Smiley and told me that if I was ready to hike on, I could go.

With that permission, I was packed up in less than three minutes and walking fast to catch with my buds. The rocky terrain was full of day hikers and section hikers. I said, "Excuse me," at least a dozen times.

I caught up with and passed Lost and Smiley just after Mount Pierce. The views from the ridge leading to Mount Washington were breathtaking, and no picture did any of the experience justice in the least. The trail crosses the Mount Eisenhower Loop Trail a couple of times before summiting Mount Franklin. Deep down I did want to hike Mount Eisenhower, but I was on a good pace to make it to Lake of the Clouds Hut in the early afternoon. This steady pace would put me at the summit of Washington to enjoy the views up there before hiking on to Mount Madison Hut.

I skipped the summit trail to Mount Monroe, as well, before circling that amazing mountain to put me in eyesight of Lake of the Clouds Hut. The hut was magic on the mountain. There were no roads leading to any of the huts I had seen thus far, but this hut was open to all of the elements. Luckily for me it was warm and sunny with little wind to hinder my summit of Mount Washington.

The Croo of LOTC hut was hanging out in the kitchen when I arrived. A Croo member, by the name Beowolf, was there, and I had heard from another someone that he was planning a thru-hike of the Pacific Crest Trail the following year. I picked his brain and mentioned to him that I would also like to attempt the 2,600 plus miles of the PCT. Beowolf mentioned a group online that he started and suggested I become a member.

"I am getting ready to go. Thanks again for the information," I said to Beowolf.

"I am heading up the mountain, too. I have to take the garbage up, and I can join you for a bit."

"Sure, that would be awesome."

Beowolf and I hiked past the sign that warns hikers not to attempt a summit of Washington in any inclement weather. Several hikers had died attempting the climb; sometimes when it looked like the weather was fine, it turned deadly. I was content with the sun and a clear forecast for my summit. I hiked pretty hard, but I could not keep up with Beowolf, whose job it was to walk several hundred feet of ascents and descents weekly. Watching him leap up the rocks toward Washington was impressive for even my hiking ability at this point.

The summit has both a road and a rail system that bring people to the mountain without breaking a sweat. Beowolf was the hiker who explained to me that these folks, known as "goofers," look at hikers like one would see an orangutan at a zoo. Some of them are, and some of them aren't. The able-bodied people I saw on the summit fitted the description, but I wasn't passing too much judgment.

The summit also has a restaurant. Several hikers and I ate an excellent meal sitting in the dining area of Mount Wash. I had a big bowl of chili with cheddar cheese, sour cream, and a big hunk of corn bread with a pop. It was not the best food, but I had just burned roughly a thousand calories getting there, so it was pretty all right.

I left the restaurant to find Smiley501, Hot Mama, and Lost-n-Found in line at the Mount Washington summit sign.

"Uke, get your picture taken with me," Lost yelled out.

"Sweet. Okay! But let's jump up ahead," I suggested, passing all the folks who drove or rode the tram to get there.

Lost and I politely passed the goofers while getting our picture took at the summit sign. It was nice getting a shot of us together, knowing we hiked together in Georgia. More like she hiked the pants off of me, but still, an excellent time on one of America's famed mountains with a very cool woman. Lost had to get off the trail for a wedding and told me that Smiley501 would hike on with me to Mount Madison Hut. I was sad that she couldn't join us, but I knew that she needed to be at an important event.

I took in the views a while longer before Smiley501, Hot Mama, and I continued toward Mount Madison Hut. The weather could not have been better, and we arrived at the hut just as the sun was setting and a glorious moon was rising between Mount Madison and another mountain I did not know. The three of us dropped seven hundred feet from Thunderstorm Junction into the welcoming building at the base of Mount Madison.

The Croo were kind enough to allow Smiley501 a space outside for Hot Mama so he could stay inside the shelter. During dinner, the Croo put on a little skit to remind the guests to pack out their trash. The guys from the Croo had on dresses and acted out an excellent theatrical skit. There was laughter, but at the end: "In all seriousness, pack out your shit!"

Smiley501 checked on Hot Mama several times throughout the night. I signed the hut log, as I had done for all the shelter logs. The cool thing about the shelter logs in the Whites is they save them all. It is like a yearbook dating back to the early 1900s in some cases. In most of them, I always would pull the year of my birth, 1977, to see what was going on. Sometimes the month would even come up, September. But rarely did I find one with the day, twenty-seventh. It was nostalgic to read back through what the hikers of the day had to experience. The entries most times would be how exhausting it was to get to the hut. Other times it would be hikers talking about cheating death. In one case a severe snowstorm and in another bugs that swarmed, almost causing hikers to fall to their deaths. In the latter, I was so happy to be hiking closer to fall with little to no bugs around me. For that, I count myself very lucky.

The next morning, I hiked out alone to summit Mount Madison just after the sun had come up. On my hike up, I met a tourist hiker from England. He and I stopped and talked for a bit. I mentioned to him that two of the coolest people I hiked with in Georgia were from England. I knew better than to give him their names.

"Hey, do you know so-and-so from London?"

"Yeah, do you know how many people are from London?"

"Oh, so you don't know them then?"

My new friend from England and I laughed at that same joke on a rock ledge below the summit of Mount Madison. We bid each other "cheers" and headed on our merry ways. So good to see people from other countries experience the positive things our nation has to offer.

The ascent of the Mountain Madison on the opposite face was ridiculous. Rock climbing has never been my bag, baby. In many instances heading down, I had to inch my butt along the sharp stone, grapple my fingers around sketchy shale, and hang on as I slid myself to firm footing. My feet and knees were yelling at me when I moved along the chest-high tree line. The scramble of rock steps went down to twenty-foot pine trees. The trail did not level off until I hit a small stream after the trail to Osgood Tent Site. I made my way down to Pinkham Notch and got a ride from a couple to a hoagie restaurant in Gorham.

Gorham was happy reunions with Chipmunk, Mama and Papa Chip, Whisper, Mamacita, and Wicked-Miner. I met Siren for the first time in Pinkham Notch. Whisper was kind enough to drive me to Maine to get a new phone because the miles were not gracious to my old one. Whisper and I had chicken wings at a local eatery after I got my phone. We drove back to Pinkham Notch, where I set my tent up behind the Chip-mobile.

My goal was to be up early the next day to hike in the difficult mountains of Wildcat Mountain Peaks E, D, C, and A. In that order. While I was sleeping soundly throughout the night, I heard a loud voice outside. A flashlight was beaming on my face through my tent walls. I was silent for a minute.

"Hello? You can't camp here! Hello?"

"Yeah, man? I am trying to sleep. I have a big day ahead of me tomorrow."

"You can't camp here. I am going to have to call the police."

"Man? All right. I'll get up."

I angrily packed up my tent and other gear for the night. It was two a.m., and there was nowhere else to go. I put my pack on and went to the visitor's center, where the restrooms were open. There were a couple of benches in the common area. I put my sleeping pad down on one of the benches and crawled into my sleeping bag. I needed to get a few more hours of sleep so that I could have an unsullied day of hiking.

Sleep came over me in my less-than-comfortable spot on the common area bench when about an hour later I heard: "Hey."

I drew my sleeping bag out and pushed my bare feet in the direction of the voice.

"Are you serious? I have to climb seven mountains tomorrow. Do you see my feet? They are sore and I don't plan on staying here but a few more hours. If you keep waking me up, it could make my hike less safe. Can you please leave me alone, and I promise I will be out of here by six a.m."

The voice came back less aggressive this time.

"Ahh, yeah. I'm sorry. I won't bother you anymore."

The guard walked away, and I came in and out of a lackluster REM of sleep. By five a.m., I was awake and ready to hike out. I went back out to the Chip-mobile, and I noticed Mama Chip.

"Hi, Uke, did you sleep well?"

I spent a few minutes explaining to her about my crazy early morning wake-up calls. She was sympathetic as I said my good-byes. The next few hours were going to test me for my continuing rock climbing ability.

The highway crossing at NH 16 was void of traffic as I traversed the concrete path. The Appalachian Trail snakes along a pond before a jettison up 851 feet in less than a half-mile to a spectacular view of the Presidential Range with Mount Washington at the helm. I caught up with Chipmunk on the steep rock ascent. She and I had a snack break and enjoyed the low-lying clouds rolling through the notch below.

We hiked together to another precipitous climb of a stone crevasse. We had to figure out the problem for a few minutes before making an attempt. She did an excellent job getting up, and I spotted her movements in case she fell while videoing her climb for her ma. I was multitasking. My legs got a little wobbly as I followed behind her up the tricky climb. "Chipmunk is a rock star," was my thought when I grabbed a handhold to pull myself to safety on the precipice.

As we exited the tree line at Wildcat Mountain Peak D, we were greeted by a large gondola and several tourists taking pictures. The comedy of the thing is she and I just busted our asses climbing to the top when we could have just paid six bucks and got to the upper part without exerting one breath. Laughable, man, which is what it was.

The last of the Wildcat Mountain Peaks was a success, as Chipmunk and I smiled, exhausted yet victorious. Chipmunk and I carefully made our descent into the last hut in New Hampshire along the Appalachian Trail, Carter Notch Hut. The Croo there was getting ready for the end of the season. There were a lot of chores to do before the helicopter came to get the supplies that were not needed out of the backcountry.

While we were conversing with the Croo and some guests, Siren came in to join our comfortable abode in the woods.

Not many paying guests were staying, and the lead Croo member informed us secretly that we would have beds to sleep in. He showed us to our quarters for the night, and Chipmunk and I went to the common area to play a game of Monopoly.

Our game was interrupted by our work-for-stay chores. Organizing things, preparing dinner, and dishwashing were some of the chores. I did a good portion of the dishes when I turned to Chipmunk, who wanted something to do.

"Do you want to do some dishes?" I asked her.

"No, but I guess I will."

Siren snapped a few pictures to send off to her ma, as she hated the chore of dishes. Chipmunk did a good job. The Croo relieved us after everything got done and we enjoyed another impressive hut meal. Honestly, I could not thank each and every one of the hut employees enough for all they do for the entire trail communities. A great service in the middle of forested wonder.

The next morning Siren, Chipmunk, and I hiked out to climb out of Carter Notch. We took first lunch on top of Carter Dome. A few clouds were rolling in on top of us while we were sitting there. Thoughts of wet rock steps did not make us want to sit around any longer. The three of us packed up and began hiking again when a fourth hiker joined our hiker progression northbound. He was an older gentleman and friendly. We were happy to have him hiking with us.

The trail became solid rock as we gingerly made our delicate descent of Mount High. Siren was first, I was right behind her, and then Chipmunk, and then our older hiker friend. We communicated with each other well on the slicker spots on the rock. As Siren took steps onto dirt from the rock scramble, we all heard him, but could not believe what we saw.

"Hold on. I'll get my first aid kit!" I yelled.

"Don't move," Siren cautioned him.

"My arm. Where are my glasses?" he moaned.

"Before you start moving around, what hurts?" I asked him.

209

"My arm, my back a little bit. I think I can move."

"No, don't move," I also cautioned

He had fallen about fifteen feet from the rock above and landed hard on a root to the dirt path mere feet from Siren. Although we cautioned him not to move, he rolled onto his back and assessed himself. After several minutes passed, we all knew that we would need to get moving if we were going to make it to Imp Campsite. The gentleman was able to stand. He had some small cuts on his arm I gave him some Band-Aids for and his glasses were a loss to the force of the fall. We were all in shock, but happy he was able to move on his own. It was the scariest moment I witnessed on the 1,877 miles of hiking to this point.

"We better get moving before dark. Are you sure you are all right?"

"Yes. I'll be okay. Go ahead. I won't be far behind, and if I don't make the shelter, I can set up my tent," he said delicately.

"Okay. Good luck."

Just as nightfall was setting in, so was the chill in the air. We arrived at the Imp Shelter and set up our sleeping pads and bags for a cold night's sleep. We all had a hot meal before bedding down for the evening. As we were eating, our hiking partner came in. Siren asked him if he needed help with anything. He assured us he was sore but uninjured. "Thank goodness," we all thought.

The next morning we all got up slowly and began our morning ritual of fueling our bodies with calories. It was frigid, and movement was essential. The time for waking up, eating, packing, and donning packs was a short interval. We all hiked out together to the summit of Mount Moriah. Then we made an imposing plunge of 3,196 feet into US 2. Mama and Papa Chip were there to greet us. We told the eerie tale of the hike the day before and let Chipmunk fill in the rest.

Siren and I went to the very comfortable Whites Mountain Hostel. My old hiking friends from my first days in Georgia, Vita-C and Snot Rocket, were working at the hostel. When we walked into the hostel, I told Vita-C about the fall our hiking friend took.

"He will need a bath of about two whole bags of Epsom salts," I suggested.

"We'll take care of him," Vita-C assured.

I had no worries about them caring for our bruised-up comrade.

Vita-C could not have picked me up without exertion when we first met, but he wanted to try now that I had lost a big portion of my body weight out on the Appalachian Trail. He counted to three, and I leaped into his arms. It was a humbling experience, having him hold me in his arms. I couldn't remember the last time someone was able to do so.

With a comfortable bed to sleep in, I lulled the night away in the best REM I had had in a long time. The next morning, Snot Rocket made a most excellent breakfast tossed down with some delicious black coffee. I procrastinated a bit when Vita-C gave me a kick in the ass I really needed.

"Get to Maine! It's right there," and he pointed his finger toward Mount Hayes.

"Thanks, man. I am going to pack up," I said with the reluctance of leaving the creature comforts of the White Mountains Hostel.

I said good-bye to everyone at the hostel and began walking up North Road to Hogan Road, which was just a gravel side road. The climb up to Mount Hayes was well maintained. A roll down and up to the summit of Cascade Mountain had a view of the last state along the Appalachian Trail, right on the top. Siren caught up to me and I asked her about Chipmunk.

"She should be right behind us."

"Cool. But this trail has been somewhat difficult terrain. I hope she can catch up."

"Me too. I think she can make it."

Siren and I hiked into Gentian Pond Shelter and Campsite to a pretty view. A few other hikers straggled in as we arranged our beds in the three-sided haven merely a five-mile hike away from the border of Maine. Although outwardly I was showing confidence and machismo, inside I was an emotional wreck. I was happy with the thirteen state accomplishment, but not sure what the future held for me; I wept in my sleeping bag during that quiet night in Gentian Pond Shelter.

Chapter TWENTY

The short, just-shy-of-five-mile hike to the New Hampshire/Maine Appalachian Trail border sign had us all smiling and thinking about camping right there. The better judgment of the group won out after we concluded our congratulatory entrance in the "you can't get there from here" state. Many times in my hike I would say, "I'm gwyne to Maine." Well, now that I was there, a heavy weight lifted off of my shoulders. "Damn, I need a beer."

Lost-n-Found and Smiley501 caught up with us at the border sign, and we hung out with them for a while. We hiked together to Full Goose Shelter and Campsite over four mountains (Mount Carlo and Goose Eye Mountain's West, East, and North Peaks), and made an approximate drop of seven hundred feet into camp. Having a familiar face from my trail beginning of Georgia in Lost-n-Found was sweet. She was encouraging and fun to be around. Smiley501, too, was a funny character. We were some strange folks out there in the woods, but we were there, and we had each other for the moment.

Mahoosuc Notch was less than two miles from our sleeping quarters for the night. This famous, most tricky, greatest, enjoyable hike was going to be a challenge. A significant challenge I was ready for. The next morning, Siren, Smiley501, Lost-n-Found, and I agreed to stick together through the rock scramble and hodgepodge of boulders through, under, and over Mahoosuc Notch. While we all were making ready to leave, a hiker, by the name of Sheppard, came into camp.

"Hey, guys! The Notch is lovely today. Are you all headed there now?"

"Yeah. It should be a rollercoaster of a time," I chimed in.

"A rollercoaster would be less effort, but be careful in there. There are some tricky spots."

Siren and Sheppard began talking about Sheppard's hiking style. He takes his truck to the trailhead, hikes in either direction that suits his fancy, and hitchhikes back to the trail. I thought that was an impressive way, but I was still sticking to my north-bound-only demeanor.

"So your truck—parked at the ME 26, then?" Siren asked Sheppard.

"Yeah, and I will hitch back to it at Pinkham Notch," Sheppard responded.

"What if I were to take your truck and park it for you?" Siren asked.

"Yeah, I think we could work something out," Sheppard kindly replied.

Siren and Sheppard worked out the logistics for a few more minutes and then Sheppard handed her his truck keys. There were some mechanical directions for her, as well, but she collected the information and solidified our ride into another awesome place.

Mahoosuc Notch was a fun hike. Smiley501 was first, and then Lost-n-Found, I was third, and Siren was directly behind me. The rock scrambles became acute in a few spots. There was a climb of about ten feet, and as I went to grab the ledge I was going to pull myself up with, I lost my grip and fell backward, almost landing on Siren's head.

"Whoa! Are you okay?" Siren asked.

"I am so sorry!" I stood and said to her.

"Uke? Are you okay?" Lost-n-Found said from above.

"Yeah, I am all right. My backpack softened my fall. I almost fell on Siren's head, though, and I feel horrible about that." I turned to Siren. "Why don't you go ahead of me? I'll catch you if you fall."

"I'll be fine," she said as she successfully climbed where I had just fallen.

My pride was a bit hurt, but I continued up, over, jumping across boulders, and smiling most of the entire 1.1-mile rock escarpment. That was fun to see we all made it safely to the other side of Bull Branch and campsite. We took a break, but again smarter heads prevailed with the deliberation of having a vehicle to shuttle us in seven miles. The only obstacle in our way was a 1,600-foot climb of Mahoosuc Arm. This proved to be somewhat more challenging than the notch. We dug in our nails, crawled, grabbed roots and tree limbs for support, and walked up a series of smooth rock balds. I commented while walking on these flat rock bare faces, "Thank goodness it is not raining. This would be a slippery mess."

The four of us made it to Sheppard's truck and waited as Siren figured out the combination of mechanical guffaw before driving to The Cabin. The Cabin in East Andover Maine is a quaint little home run by two friendly people, named Honey and Bear.

Sheppard's truck pulled up to The Cabin, and we all got out, introducing ourselves to our hosts, Honey and Bear. They explained the rates and an added cost for a home-cooked meal. Smiley501, Lost-n-Found, and I got the bunk plus dinner. Siren had to drive to pick up a new backpack and was afraid she wouldn't make it back in time, so she just got a bunk.

Bear showed us around their establishment and explained common area rules. We all wanted to launder our clothes and shower before dinner. Many hostel businesses that run within an adventurer community have "loaner clothes" for their guests to wear while their dirty clothes get cleaned. Many hikers only carry a limited amount of materials, due to added weight in their backpacks. I was no exception.

I looked through the clothes and found a pair of 32" x 32" jeans and a size large wrestling shirt to put on after my shower. Wearing those clothes was strange because I hadn't worn those sizes since I was a junior in high school.

The bottom floor had three main rooms: a living room with a TV, a kitchenette, and the hiker dorm with several bunk beds. The upstairs was Honey and Bear's living quarters they shared with hikers over home cooked meals. As soon as I finished my shower, I walked upstairs and asked if there was anything I could do to help. Honey told me to help with some dinner prep, but not too much as she wanted me to relax, as well.

My favorite baseball team was playing a critical game that evening. I knew that this game was going to be emotional for me and instructed my fellow hikers not to join "unless you don't mind watching a grown man cry. Watching the game with me might be waterfalls for me." They laughed and assured me that I would have the TV room to myself for the playoff game. My team had not been in the playoffs since I was in the eighth grade of junior high. I watched those games with several family members who were no longer living. This game was as important to me as walking from Georgia to Maine, well.

The dinner table was set, and Lost-n-Found, Smiley501, and I were biting at the bit to get our appetite quenched. The meal consisted of fresh corn on the cob, an amazing garden salad, and a homemade chicken potpie that melted in our mouths.

After dinner, we helped clean up a bit before heading downstairs to prepare for bed. Although I was staying up for the baseball game, I made my bed for when it was time for sleepy time station.

By the fourth inning, my boys were leading 5–1. I sat there in high spirits as my eyes began to well up, thinking of the time spent with my grandparents in their living room of Emporium, Pennsylvania. In the small downstairs room of The Cabin, a grown man wept in the darkness, except for the image of the players jumping around in triumph with an end score of 6–2.

I snapped the TV off and sat for a while in total darkness before heading to the next room to sleep. I tried to hush as I walked into the bunk room. In the complete darkness, I ran into the wall with a loud "thud." I apologized in a whisper as I lay down on the bed, my eyes still wet from the emotions that emptied out of me.

I slept well that night without wakefulness or disturbances of any kind. With a fresh new day ahead, hiking in the wilds of Maine, my whole spirit roared renewed.

Chapter TWENTY-ONE

My friend Ryan and I were in contact for my summit date of Mount Katahdin. Ryan and his father-in-law, Scott, were interested in summiting the great mountain with me. I made it to Maine; I was more than happy with my accomplishments to this point in the trail.

Did I deserve to drink my hoppy goodness before completing every mile of the Appalachian Trail? This question pounded in the back of my head as I discussed the dates when Ryan was available to drive up from Emporium. I was eager to have this experience with him. I wanted him to encounter the great mountain with me, so I told him I would get back to him and let him know.

Whisper was helping Mailman, Stretch, Little Bear, and Siren with logistics on the completion of Maine. I discussed with her my dilemma on summiting Katahdin before completing the Appalachian Trail. She was helpful in not only encouraging the idea of summiting with my best friend but also with shuttling me around to make sure I accomplished the plan.

I hiked from The Cabin and ran into Miller Miller, Beeline, Schnitzel, and other hikers across Baldpate West and East Peaks. The views of the fall foliage just beginning the transition from summer was classic. A few of us enjoyed another night at The Cabin after hiking over Dunn Notch, over Wyman Mountain, through Sawyer Notch, up to Moody Mountain, Old Blue Mountain, and Beamis Mountain before hitting ME 11. We called up Bear, and he agreed to shuttle us back to The Cabin for another loosening up the night of solitude.

I spoke with Ryan about meeting in Stratton, Maine, to take us to Millinocket for the weekend of October fourth. Whisper picked me up at ME 4 near Rangeley. From there she was kind enough to take me to the hostel in Stratton to wait for Ryan the next morning. Our goal was to drive up to Millinocket on Saturday and summit on Sunday, October sixth.

Ryan and Scott arrived in Stratton, and we enjoyed some dinner before heading up the road to the Big K. We went over the details of proper hydration and maintaining a safe pace for all of us to enjoy the mountain without trying to kill ourselves.

My cousin, Jennifer, sent me a six-pack of a hoppy, barley concoction with a recipe that dates back over one hundred years. Beer—I hadn't had one of those since sitting with Larry and his friend, Bill. Bill had stopped over to tell us about his son needing boots in Connecticut for the Appalachian Trail.

The wheels that were set in motion just a little over a year and a month prior. Jennifer could not have sent me that hoppy goodness if not for my cousin's wife, Gretchen, picking it up for me in Arlington, Virginia.

Katahdin Mountain is in Baxter State Park among towering trees, mainly spruce. Ryan, Scott, and I and arrived before the sun came up on October sixth. There was a line of cars at the gate before the park opened. Ryan parked not far from the AT, where we geared up and began hiking toward the mount. I carried the six-pack of glorious nectar in my pack. A sign-in and register was posted to let the park managers know who and how many people were attempting the summit for each day. It also had a sign-in for finishing, notifying the authorities that each person was safe.

A gradual climb across a footbridge and Katahdin Stream led the three of us to a set of steps. The foliage was magnificent in reds, browns, and greens. A set of well-maintained steps led a switchback of precarious rock climbs and boulder problems. We pulled ourselves hand over hand past a small slab cave, known only as "The cave." More than 1,600 feet of continued rock scramble and appreciated rebar placing brought the three of us to The Gateway or The Tableland.

The hike above the tree line felt like being in a very slow elevator. For each one hundred feet, we would pause and look out over an expanse of Maine very few people on earth get to witness. Once we cleared the first of the massive rock steps to Thoreau Springs, I was on a tear.

Something grabbed me and pulled me. I didn't know how far behind Ryan and Scott were, but when I saw the iconic Katahdin sign, I was in a stride of magnetic proportions. I reached the sign and felt the internal emotion from a great adventure many assumed I would fail. There were about forty people on the summit. Many day hikers were out enjoying the beautiful weather and light winds. I stepped up to the sign and kissed it with my tongue. I French-kissed that sign until I formed splinters all over my mouth, in my mind. In reality, I just gave it a long lips-pressed-to-wood kiss.

Although I had 220 miles left to hike, I would not have chosen a better day I was about to experience with every person on top of the mountain. The weather was similar to my hike to the summit of Mount Washington. The temperature was about seventy, with the wind about five miles per hour. Life was most certainly real.

Ryan and Scott were approaching the summit when I saw a familiar face.

"Som' Peach?" I shouted.

"Uke? No, it's Yote!"

"No shit! Yote! What are the odds that I would summit with you?"

I knew Yote from my first day on the Appalachian Trail; he hiked with me during my spider bites, and now he enjoyed the spoils of struggle in a place where it is required to walk a treacherous piece of trail. No cars and no trains can drive to the apex of Katahdin. That, in and of itself, is pretty awesome.

Yote and I made our way to the sign, where I cracked a few cold beers for my first taste of the hoppy, barley sauce since late August 2012. The sparks of synapses during that first tablespoon of beer on my lips were orgasmic. No, really . . . they were. There are not even words in Mandarin Chinese to describe the feeling I was having in that luxurious moment. The time and distance it took to acquire that exact sensation will be very difficult for me to duplicate in my lifetime.

Roadkill and Cheers were coincidentally also on the mount. (They were dubbed "The Rescue Team" after the time they headed out in the Vermont darkness to find Ryan.) Acorn, the amazing woman whom I met crushing miles before the Nantahala Outdoor Center, arrived a while after I had. We all talked about life and trail stuff with enthusiasm and awe.

Roadkill brought her ukulele, too, and she played a song she had written about her trail experience. Each of us had the most genuine smiles on that October sixth day in the Year of Our Lord, 2013.

Ryan, Scott, and I had a nice lunch and enjoyed the astonishing views of the Maine valleys, mountains, and rolling hills. The trees were in full autumn color. We counted ourselves lucky to be living in that moment for a while before agreeing to get back down to the car.

Ryan invited Yote and a trail friend, Papa Smurf, to dinner that evening. The five of us filled our gullets with an all-you-can-eat Chinese buffet. Scott and Ryan observed three long-distance hikers reminisce about experiences with so many wonderful humans throughout the diverse AT obstacles that we encountered.

Chapter TWENTY-TWO

Ryan and Scott dropped me off at Rangeley, Maine, where Whisper picked me up a few days prior. I thanked them again for such an awesome experience and said how I was pleased they could have that event with me.

The next trek over Saddleback Mountain at 4,120 feet was met with an exhaustive gale force wind and hail-induced grunt of a hike. The winds and I had a good go of it for the while. I screamed, "Stop it!" with added expletives as the gusts drove me backward. I cleared the mountain but was still in whipping clouds around me as I punched over The Horn and Saddleback Junior.

In the darkness, my path illuminated by my headlamp, I arrived at Poplar Ridge Lean-to, where my worn and tired body moved within a vacuum to accomplish my bedtime tasks.

The next morning I was moving a bit timidly. Time was passing by quickly on my walk through the powerful currents of Orberton Stream, a steady pace over Lone Mountain, nipping the shoulder of Spaulding Mountain, and down to the South Branch of the Carrabassett River. My thoughts continued to wander as fast as my steps.

The more I walked, the more I thought about where my life was heading. For now, my life was fording yet another steady, current-filled stream of the Carrabassett. The water was clear, fresh. The air was crisp, new. There was a hiker who was lost in the area I was now in while I was hiking in southern Pennsylvania. As I walked through the river's current, she had yet to be found. Chills ran up my spine, thinking perhaps she lost her balance and was swept downstream where I was looking at that exact moment. The feeling was eerie, and I wanted to be as far away as possible from that river and the horrible thoughts of what might have happened. She was still lost; I said a prayer for her before I stepped my soaking feet on the bank of the opposite side of the Carrabassett.

A steady climb of South and North Crocker Mountains brought me back to the trail at ME 27 and the road leading into Stratton. I crossed the highway, and my uninterrupted steps moved me up to the Bigelow Range and a beautiful skyline.

The trail remained strenuous with an ascent of almost three thousand feet to the west peak of the Bigelow Mountains. A dive of roughly the same elevation took me over Avery Peak and the flat top of Little Bigelow Peak until I was safely in camp at West Carry Pond Lean-to.

It was a strange feeling hiking by myself to the waters of the great Kennebec River. This river is about thirty yards wide and very deep. Some hikers who choose to ford it by swimming across its dangerous currents, in my opinion, are hardcore. Good fortune, in the guise of a manned canoe, had me across promptly to hike on to Pleasant Pond Lean-to.

My cousins, Jennifer, Robby, and Lucas, were meeting me in Bar Harbor for a celebratory get together after my hike. I did not sleep well at Pleasant Pond, so I woke up and night walked into Monson. A 27.7-mile crushing had me watching the sunrise over Lake Hebron.

I enjoyed Monson and witnessed a beautiful sunset on the lake before going off to bed to rest before heading into the One Hundred Mile Wilderness. Knowing that my cousins were waiting for me at a cabin in Bar Harbor, I hiked out as hard as I could. The trail meandered through streams, mud, thick hardwood forests, and over one thousand feet of the Barren Mountain.

I enjoyed myself very much through the wilderness and spent both alone time and time with some pretty cool hiker trash folks. This experience taught me to slow down and observe more. Show acts of love instead of hate. I learned to abstain from things I love, create goals, and get the reward of the love object after the goal. I also learned the love of both family and friends. My crazy ass could not have gone as far as I did on the Appalachian Trail had it not been for them. I was a man on a mission, *Hiking to Beer*!

Acknowledgments

There is a multitude of people I want to thank:

First I would like to thank my mother and my father, Doreen Harris and Lloyd L. Fink Sr., for bringing me into this world.

Also, I have to thank my mom and dad, Bob and Doreen Harris, who raised me in my adolescence. That was not easy, let me tell you. The Magaro family: when all seemed lost for me as a young, disjointed, wild kid, you all were there for me when I needed support and encouragement to chive on.

This may sound odd, but I would like to thank my probation officer during my adolescence, Jan Burkness. See, I didn't turn out all that bad.

And, of course, to my family no longer here with us, I would like to thank my grandparents, Anna and Homer Picklesimer, for having some of the best family meals I will never forget. Dale and Roger Secco, my uncles, for showing that even though life can bring us down at times, perseverance goes a long way.

This journey of over two thousand miles from Georgia to Maine was a task I could not have done without words of encouragement, trail packages of the most wonderful goodness, and cash . . . cash, the unfortunate king:

Doreen and Bob Harris
Ginger and Timothy Thomas
Jennifer and Robby Schwartz

Joyce "Mom Mom" Schwartz

Greg Magaro

Ryan and Brandi Magaro

Lucas Schwartz

Adrienne and Chris Rouette

Shelly Gore

The Zoschg Family (Megan Canniere)

Miss Janet Hensley

Ed Fink

Sarah Jennings

Larry Hinkle

Robyn Schwartz

Tammy and Jason Warren

Alex Baumgardner and family

Christopher Thomas and Gretchen Stelgar

TJ Schwartz

Jamie Harrell and Matt Potter

Kate Waite

Kathleen Kolos

Jake Jenson

Terry Jones

Jim Garrett

Teresa Louise

Tonya and Dean Hamilton

Lloyd L. Fink Sr.

Neil Gerstenmeir

Greg and Mary Secco

Travis Secco

Amy Hepner

Tina Lydon

Nicole Mannan

Rach and Bridget

Michael Leavitt

CPSIA information can be obtained
at www.ICGtesting.com
Printed in the USA
LVHW062026200119
604185LV00004BA/4/P